BYGONE DAYS IN CAMBUSBARRON

BYGONE DAYS IN CAMBUSBARRON

By
P. T. Paterson

STIRLING DISTRICT LIBRARIES
and
CAMBUSBARRON COMMUNITY COUNCIL

First published 1980
reprinted 1993

ISBN 1 870542 23 1

Published by
Stirling District Libraries
Stirling

Printed by
Cordfall Ltd
041 332 4640

CONTENTS

The Brae, Cambusbarron.

FOREWORD

"The plesandness and amenitie of the fields
and healthsumnes of the Air."
(from a 1641 reference to Cambusbarron)

This guide is intended as a modest introduction to Cambusbarron's past. As such , it makes no claims to deep scholarship, academic detachment or the scientific methodology of the trained historian. Certainly some primary sources, principally at Scottish Records Office and New Register House, Edinburgh, and Central Region's Archives Department in Stirling, yielded much fascinating information. So, also, however, did the many conversations with older villagers, letters from exiles, past numbers of local papers and the myriad scraps of knowledge culled from a variety of printed sources, from the modest "History of the Cooperative Society in Stirling" to the monumental "Edinburgh History of Scotland". To all who helped with the first edition – the Scottish Arts Council, the Central Regional Council, Cambusbarron Community Council, our local archivists and librarians I offer my gratitude. For the encouragement and help to produce a second edition I must thank Stirling District Libraries and my local Community Council. The contribution of Mr. George Waller, Principal Teacher of Art, St. Modan's High School, Stirling, who was responsible for the cover illustrations is also gratefully recorded. And thanks also to the many non-specialists, most from Cambusbarron, who supplied information, documents, photographs and clerical assistance.

Exploring the past is both agreeable and hazardous: agreeable because it's that place where the long-silent generations may come to life again, hazardous, because it's easy to get it wrong. I've tried not to, of course, but should flawed reasoning or faulty judgement or plain inaccuracy rear their unpleasant heads, I ask forbearance, as I do also for any village toe trodden upon in this narrative. (It was not intended. In similar vein, with some exceptions, I have been reluctant to cover the years after 1918; they are still too close to us).

A final plea: few are given the opportunity to wax lyrical in print on a subject close to the heart – so I've taken full advantage. Please forgive the prejudices and purple patches. I hope that the pages that follow will go some way to paint in the backcloth of our modern village. The pleasure, if not the privilege, of spending our days in such congenial surroundings, is only enhanced by a knowledge of their past.

~1~

PREHISTORY

On a cold February morning in 1879, work was brought to a halt at Drummond's Coney Park Nursery, Cambusbarron. Some of the men digging through a mound of earth in the centre of the nursery, had struck an obstacle. When they cleared back the soil, the gardeners discovered several stones placed against and over each other as if to form a small wall sealed by a yellowish clay the Coneypark men had not seen before in their nursery. And when they broke through this mound the men were astonished at what they found: a human skeleton. It was propped against the inside wall. It had been there for 2,500 years. And as fresh air displaced the fetid atmosphere of the tomb, and the intruders stood transfixed, the skeleton disintegrated before their eyes.

Through its circumstances were fairly dramatic, this find, the tomb of some important person, *(Map Reference* 783926) was only one of several made in the locality during the second half of the nineteenth century which suggest that some kind of community was already established in Cambusbarron during the Bronze Age - from 1700 to 500 B.C., in the Stirling area. At least four other cists - a cist being a tomb consisting of a stone chest covered with stone slabs - were found in the stretch of land between Birkhill and the Kings Park: two were discovered in the garden of Birkhill House (780926 and 779926), one containing bones and an ornamental urn, possibly a food vessel; a partly destroyed cist was found in Birkhill sand-pit (779925), and a broken urn in the sand-pit and adjoining Douglas Terrace (782920). Besides these cist finds, several other pieces of Bronze Age pottery have been discovered in the Cambusbarron area, including beakers and cinerary urns (i.e. urns containing ashes of the dead). Unfortunately, the exact circumstances surrounding these discoveries, perhaps as many as ten, have not been recorded, though most of the relics are preserved in either the Smith Institute or the National Museum of Antiquities in Edinburgh.

A final interesting, if enigmatic, Bronze Age relic is the cup-and-ring marking in the Kings Park where it overlooks the village. This consists of a natural stone marked by what appears to be a cup $1^{1/2}$ inches in diameter and $^{1/2}$ inch deep surrounded by a ring 5 inches in diameter and $^{1/4}$ inch deep. Last officially inspected in 1958, it was then described as being near the summit of the crag that borders the Park and lies behind Douglas Terrace, some 45 yards east of a seat on the summit. The map reference is 783930, but the hopeful searcher will have much difficulty in discovering its whereabouts due to the thick growth of turf and bushes in the area. Its significance, like others found throughout the British Isles and the continent, remains a mystery though one theory suggests that the markings may symbolise the sun (cup) and its heat (ring) and that they were produced in connection with the activities of the Bronze Age smiths and smelters.

About the earlier inhabitants of Cambusbarron before the Bronze Age dwellers, little is known and we have to rely even more on inference and guess work. After the Ice Age, some 8,000 years ago, some areas of present day Cambusbarron were under water - part of the great post-glacial flood created by the melting of the ice; the River Forth is a modern descendant of that sea. Much of the flat, low-lying land is a noticeable feature of the Forth Valley, both to the east and west of Stirling once formed the bed of this great sea loch. Numerous fish fossils and remains have been recorded in the area, the most interesting of which was the 50 ft. skeleton of a whale found at West Carse on Touch estate during the construction of the present Dunbarton Road in the early years of last century. The present Touch Road, in fact, as it leaves the village from the West End, follows the line of the prehistoric raised beach of the Forth, and a great, semi-circular bay was once formed behind Touch House, Gartur House and Hillhead Farm.

From approximately 3,000 B.C. the water gradually receded until by Christian times it had reached the present shoreline of the Forth. And it is the carse clay of the one-time sea that has provided evidence of the earliest human presence in the Stirling area in the form of primitive tools made from bone and antlers. "Kitchen middens" alongside testify to the diet of these people of the Mesolithic Period ("Meso - lithic" - middle stone age, i.e. they lived 3,500 years ago): mussels, cockles, periwinkles and whelks, fish and perhaps the occasional luxury of a stranded whale. A heavy round stone with a hole in the middle, unearthed by Mr. W. McEwan a few years ago from the fields of his Hillhead Farm, may well be a net-sinker used by these early fishermen. A barked flint arrow-head from Murrayshall Lime Kilns in 1911, a clay-stone axe from Whitehouse Farm in 1893 and an axe-head from Greystale Farm in 1880 are the only other recorded finds in the locality which may date from Stone Age times.

Whether or not Stone Age Man settled for any length of time in what is now Cambusbarron, is impossible to say. It may well be that, driven to ensure a steady food supply, he was nomadic and, living in rough brush-wood and reeded huts or tents, he wandered up and down the southern shoreline of the prehistoric Forth.

The first farmers, possibly the forefathers of those who left the Coneypark and Birkhill relics, came to the area in approximately 3,000 B.C., coinciding with the receding waters of the Forth. Attracted by lighter sands and gravel which supported a more open vegetation cover than the heavier, if ultimately more productive, clay soil, these early farmers ignored both the re-emerging carse lands – in later centuries to become some of the best farmland in Scotland– and the more exposed uplands, to settle on the lower, better-drained hill slopes of the region, on

land such as that around Cambusbarron and, in particular, that of the Touch area which has up to fairly recent times supported a number of farms. Not until the invention of the heavy plough in the Iron Age did the farmers move down to the carse. The dwellings of these people, though still extremely primitive, were more permanent than the wattle and daub huts of their predecessors, and consisted of a singular rectangular room with stone and mud walls and a thatched roof held up by central timber posts. At one end there would be a door, but no windows, the only outlet being in the centre of the roof for smoke from the fire. Unfortunately, no finds of such dwelling places have been made in our area though they are recorded elsewhere.

A third phase in the prehistory of the Cambusbarron area is marked by a number of Iron Age sites, particularly of the hill fort and dun variety which are found exclusively to the west and south west of the village. That no such remains are presently known inside the village itself does not preclude their earlier existence: their sites may have been built upon over the centuries or have been destroyed by the plough or - a common fate for many ancient monuments - they may have been quarries for later builders and their material plundered. A fourth possibility is that the comparatively more gentle slopes of Cambusbarron did not impress the builders of these duns and forts as having the same forbidding defensive qualities as the clifftops and steep summits of the Murrayshall, Sauchie Crags and Gillies Hill areas.

It is on the west-facing crag of Gillies Hill that is recorded the nearest of these hill forts[1] to the village. It lay just back from the cliff face at a point where the crags are interrupted by a transverse gully (769917).

The other Gillies Hill site is the Wallstale Dun (774909) which lies on a south-projecting spur of the woodland 160 yards north of Wallstale Farm. This was once known to local people as "The Temple" and was a favourite picnic spot in Victorian days.

Duns were generally smaller than hill forts and, varying greatly in size and shape, date of construction and duration of occupation, seem to have been used for defence. They were distinguished by their comparatively small size and disproportionately thick walls.

Today's interested antiquarian, however, is inevitably disappointed when he arrives at one of the sites: due to extensive quarrying by later generations, the duns and hill forts have lost most of their stonework and it is often difficult to imagine them as they once were.

With one notable exception, this is true of the remaining sites in the Murrayshall/ Sauchie/Touch area: there is Wester Craigend, or Sauchie Fort, (767906) lying approximately 360 yards west of Craigend House, on the high cliffs above the Bannockburn (or Limestone Burn, as it has been known to generations of Cambusbarron people); Touchadam Fort, (767909) now merely a rocky mound just to the north of Limestone Road at the entrance of Murrayshall Farm. This site was known by locals in Victorian times as "The Camp"; the Touch Muir Dun, in open moorland which descends gradually southwards to the left bank of the upper reaches of the West Burn 30 yards away. It is 770 yards N.N.W. by N. of what was once the boathouse of No.4 loch, Touch Muir. It is 42 ft. in diameter and a ruined stone wall varying in thickness between 8 and 12 ft. is now a grass banking though the eastern entrance is well defined; there are two dun sites on the Castlehill area of Touch, the first (766908) on a rocky outcrop 760 yards S.E. of the ruins of Castlehill Farmhouse. All the stones were removed last century. The second (760909) is on a rocky knoll a quarter of a mile south of the same ruined farmhouse.

Four other prehistoric sites in this area, though not apparently duns or hill forts, should be recorded. One is Woodside Homesteads (753912) and this lies in the uppermost of the cultivated fields of Woodside Farm some 650 yards S.W. of this Farmhouse. It is D-shaped in plan and is 170 ft. in length E. to W. A group of small huts would have stood within the boundaries of the homestead and the stone foundations of two may still be observed. The second is described by the Royal Commission of Ancient Monuments as a "Mound at Touch" (750931) lying beside the farm road running south from the former West Lodge of Touch, 300 yards from that building. It may be a denuded cairn. Thirdly there is an enclosure on Touch Muir, consisting now of only a few boulders, 100 yards W.N.W. from Touch Muir Dun, near the West Burn (722920). And finally indeterminate

ruins (749930) have been found on open ground 400 yards south of Touch West Lodge. They may be the remains of an ancient farmhouse.

The most impressive Iron Age site in the area is, however, the dun at Castlehill Wood. This lies 1,100 yards W.S.W. of the ruins of the Castlehill Farmhouse and is oval shaped, measuring 75 ft. from N.E. to S.W. by 50 ft. transversely within a dry stone dyke 6 ft. thick situated at a height of 650 ft. above sea-level, the dun commands a fine view of the surrounding countryside and its original occupants would have been able to maintain visual contact with most of the other forts in the area. Remains of fires have been found, as have various small artifacts which suggest that occupants lived in the adjacent area, possibly in wattle and daub shelters. More interestingly, fragments of Roman glass have also been uncovered, dating the structure to the first or second century A.D. and suggesting that the invading Romans may have taken temporary occupation of the fort; alternatively, the fragments may be the result of invader/native trade or battle plunder.

The Romans themselves have left almost no traceable impact on Cambusbarron. A local 19th Century tradition that Birkhill House was built on the site of a Roman villa seems unlikely; a record of fragments of a Roman urn being found in Cambusbarron Sandpit, formerly to the west of Birkhill House, may have more validity or may be the result of confusion with Bronze Age relics there; and the 1841 Statistical Account suggestion that the foundations of a road uncovered at Bearside Farm in the 1830s was Roman, is now regarded as doubtful, though the Account contended that the road might lead to Castlehill Dun or to a ford over the Forth at Kildean. (More recent research suggests that the main Roman road north came through St. Ninians then veered slightly to the west of Stirling through Laurelhill Place and Snowdon Place, and then probably to Kildean.

The Iron Age duns and hill forts are the final remnants of Cambusbarron's prehistory. In fact, spanning as they do they gulf between BC and AD they are bridges in time between the distant days of our earliest ancestors, and the beginnings of what we regard as recorded history. Despite the ravages of the intervening millennia, these very old stones, ancient relics of Cambusbarron's earliest days, profoundly affect the imagination; we think of their silent survival over the centuries, the lost worlds that surged and fell around them, and most of all, of the people who left them.

1 The future of this site is threatened by a possible extension of workings Murrayshall Quarry. A planning application for such extension is present being considered by Stirling District Council.

Village boys during World War I, preparing to help get in the harvest. (Most able-bodied men were in the Forces).

~2~

BANNOCKBURN AND THE CHAPELWELL

On the steep south-facing crag of the Gillies Hill, there stood, up to a few years ago when it eventually succumbed to the ever-inward gulpings of Murrayshall Quarry, an ancient Scots pine. To more than one generation of Cambusbarron folk, this was the "Bonnety Tree" so called because it was here, the story went, that the camp followers, servants or "gillies" of Bruce's army hung their bonnets prior to their dramatic intervention in the Battle of Bannockburn in June, 1314.

The story was one that every local school child knew well: how, at a crucial stage in the battle, with its outcome in the balance, these gillies, "armed" only with pots, pans and other kitchen utensils, marched around the slopes of the hill above Cambusbarron to the battlefield. To the hard-pressed English forces the frying pans glinting in the sun looked like swords and pikes, and the war-like screams and shouts of those brandishing them seemed to be the battle cries of some fresh and confident Scots army, deliberately held in reserve until that moment. The morale of the invaders broke, the tide of battle moved with the Scots, and the rest, as it is often said, is history.

The "Bonnety Tree" story, charming though it is, and important as part of the folk-lore of our area, rests on dubious historical ground. The significance of the gillies' contribution to the battle may also have been exaggerated in the popular imagination down the centuries. More reasonable is the claim that the camp followers were stationed in Cambusbarron and made their way to the battlefield from there: the huge hill around which they village has grown has been known as the Gillies Hill for a very long time, certainly long before the local authority gave

that name in the 1940s to what had become the longest street in the village. And John Barbour, the poet, writing a century after the battle, tells in his epic poem *The Bruce* how the king. . .

> Syne all the small folk and vital
> He sent with harnes and victual
> Into the park, well far him fra,
> And fra the battles gart them ga;
> They held their way to a valley
> Out of the fight of the battaley'.

The valley most convenient for accommodating a large number of people, yet sufficiently distant for safety, was that of Cambusbarron. Certainly, if we believe the most famous legend of Cambusbarron's links with the battle, the story of Bruce and the Chapelwell –then it is clear that the King would have had some knowledge of the terrain in and around the village.

The story is that on the eve of the battle – both a personal crisis for Bruce and a national one for his country – the King sought religious comfort at the chapel of Cambusbarron. This small building, a satellite of the more important Cambuskenneth Abbey, lay in the small valley called Glenmoray, on the bank of a stream of the same name (Glenmoray Burn) in what is now known as the Chapelcroft or Chapelwell area of the village.

It was here then that Bruce came on 23rd June, 1314, to take the sacrament and to drink from the well of the Chapel. From the well also was taken by Bruce's religious adviser, the Abbot Maurice of Inchaffray, the holy water that was sprinkled on the field before battle in the hope of victory.

As a result of this link with the King and the successful outcome of the visit to the Chapel and

Well, there arose a belief in the minds of ordinary folk that the water of the spring was invested with supernatural qualities and the Well thereafter became a place of pilgrimage for local people. Many visited the shrine hoping for relief from pain and suffering or a cure for blindness or lameness. By the 17th century such visits had become so popular – particularly on days that harked back to pre-Christian times – e.g. May Day, Beltane – that they incurred the disapproval of the local Kirk Session, sensitive in the religiously turbulent post-Reformation Scotland, to anything smacking of Catholicism.

On July 12, 1610, for example, it is recorded that:

"The quhilk day comperit Grissal Glen and Marioun Gillaspie quha for ther superstitione in passing in pilgrimmage to 'Christe's Well' as they confessit the last day ar ordeinit to mak publick repentance the next Sunday in lining claithis"

and on June 1st, 1630 that

"The quhilk day comperit Elspet Aiken, spous to Andro Cuyngham, tinckler, Jonet Harvie, William Huttoune, cutler; Margaret Mitchell, dochter to Alex. Mitchell; Jonet Bennet, dochter to James Mitchell, cuik; James Ewein, son of John Ewein, wobster; Margaret Wight, James Watsoune, who confessis passing in pilgrimage to 'Christe's Well' in Mai, and thairfoir they ar ordeaned to mak publick repentance the nixt Sabbat in thair awin habeit, under the paine of disobedience.

Lykway I, Mr. Patrik Bell, am ordeaned to desyre the breithren of the Presbyterie to appoint ane actual minister for to preach upon Sonday nixt for to tak ordour with the said personnes above written."

and on October 6th, 1631 that

"Jonet Norbell, in Cambusbarron, for going for water to help her sick son; and Jonet Main in Cambusbarron, going to 'Christe's Well' for water to help her bairns; and for another offence are ordained 'to sair the pulpit on Sonday nixt in her ain habit to mak repentance."

The twenty-one years between the first and last

of these declarations of official disapproval testify to the powerful impression made by the well on the imagination of ordinary people. "Christe's Well", as the spring was by this time known, then fades into history along with the chapel. We know that in the early years of the 19th century, the then owner of the land on which the now ruinous chapel was sited, a Mr. Rennie, reduced the remaining walls to rubble in the anticipation – deservedly unfulfilled, a contemporary observer smugly notes – of finding any long-hidden treasure. The cast-down stones were then appropriated by locals and used in the building of new dwellings in the village. No trace of the chapel is today visible in the Chapelcroft area though interestingly, two "gargoyles", as they were called by villagers, were once a prominent feature of "The Barns", a building demolished in the 1950's, which stood in the open ground at the junction of Mill Road and North End. One of these gargoyles appears to have at some time fallen from the wall and broken; the other now forms part of an ornamental wall in the garden on the nearby Alma House and, though much eroded by weather, a human form is still just recognisable. Could this be a surviving remnant of Cambusbarron's ancient chapel?

The Well continued to be used as a domestic water supply until the end of last century. Originally consisting of a square stone opening with parapets and a large basin, it was eventually closed and bricked up by the local authority as a health risk. The Well then gradually disappeared from memory – and sight – as earth and rubbish piled up and covered it (the site seems to have been a temporary midden) until by recent years only the more senior villagers could recall its existence. However, an initiative in 1979 by Cambusbarron Community Council has led to the re-discovery and restoration of the Well and the intention is that a plaque recording its history will be placed on the sight [1.]

Another plaque – bronze and not the synthetic material of more modern times – was discovered some years ago by a keeper in Polmaise Woods just above the Castle and this is believed to be the seal of one David Austin of Inverness who was possibly with Bruce's forces at the Battle. An ancient spur, dug up at the Castle Lodge in 1915, may also be a remnant from 1314.

Bruce's visit to Cambusbarron is also commemorated in the name of our village church, the full title of which is "Cambusbarron, the Bruce Memorial Church". This name was suggested by Dr. John Saunders Muschett of Birkhill, a Victorian gentleman who owned considerable land in the village including the Chapelcroft. Anxious to redress the vandalism of his predecessor who had pulled down the remaining walls of the chapel, the Doctor was prominent in a campaign for a new church to be built, Cambusbarron at this time having no purpose-built building. A considerable sum was raised by subscription and an eminent architect, Mr. Rockhead, actually drew up the plans. (The same Mr. Rockhead who was responsible for the Wallace Monument; one wonders what kind of structure we would have had at the end of the Main Street today if the project had come to fruition). The enterprise, however, did not succeed but the Doctor's intention to preserve the memory of Bruce's visit to Cambusbarron Chapel was realised long after his death, the church being built in 1910 [2] and taking the title suggested by Dr. Muschett.

The village, incidentally, owes a debt of gratitude to the present minister, the Rev. W. Craig and his session board who recently (1976) asserted the claim of Cambusbarron Church to be known as "The Bruce Memorial" when there was an attempt by the Presbytery of Stirling to describe it by the bare "Cambusbarron Church".

After the battle, it was said, many of the illustrious dead were interred in the Chapel burial ground which was, after all, consecrated earth, and the Statistical Account of 1841 records that human remains had been periodically unearthed in what by that time had become domestic gardens. In 1892, workmen digging out the founds of an underground cellar for Cullens, the local butchers, unearthed nine human skeletons, some of which were well over six feet in height. This latter detail confirmed in the minds of villagers at the time that the belief that remains were those of English nobility

Today, despite its location in the centre of the village and proximity to busy roads, the Chapelcroft is a peaceful and sequestered spot, with the distinctive atmosphere that all ancient places share. Long may it flourish.

1   This, in fact, has been done. A plaque donated by Central Regional Council was unveiled on Friday, 30th November, 1979 – St. Andrew's Day – by Mrs. E. Graham, a lifelong history enthusiast.

2   For the history behind this enterprise, see Chapter 8.

~3~

FRAGMENTS

Besides the Chapelwell, several other springs helped to form the medieval landscape of Cambusbarron. That of St. Thomas's is probably the best-known today, largely because it is one of the few to have preserved both well and title. The origins of the name, however, are lost in antiquity though one possibility – stemming from the finely-dressed stones used to form the walls of outhouses when the present buildings were erected in 1828 – is that a church dedicated to St. Thomas once stood on the site.

"The Bog Well" in its final days stood on the right hand (southern) side of the Mill Road as it leads towards the mill from North End Road. Originally this spring emerged in one of the fields of St. Thomas's Farm, several hundred yards away, but in Victorian times a dispute arose between villagers and the then farmer over a possible right of way to the spring. To prevent further encroachment on his land, the owner had the water piped to its Mill Road site, where it acquired its name from the marshy nature of the surrounding field.

Another ancient well, designated "holy" and now lost, was that of St. Corbet – possibly St. Cuthbert – which was sited in Touch Glen not far from the attractive waterfall called Gilmour's Linn. St. Corbet's Well – even as comparatively recently as the beginning of the 19th century – attracted the more impressionable young people in the village for at least one hour every year: that before sunrise on the first Sabbath in May. The reward for the early morning walker was not only a drink of deliciously cold water but also, according to superstition, immunity from death during the ensuing twelve months.

In passing it is interesting to note that local superstition was powerful enough to survive as late as 1897 when, after the death of a local clergyman, the Rev. George Williams, his relatives were visited by a village woman with the request to "give me something o' his tae keep me from dreaming about him, an't but a lead pencil".

An earlier reference (1852) claims the village to have been a favourite haunt of witches during the reign of James VI and insists "that at no time since has it lost its demoniacal association". One elderly lady, a "Widow Dunn", gained a reputation for witchcraft with an interesting line in metamorphosis: she would apparently turn into an owl and attack her enemies from the air.

The Fir Park Boiling Springs are now sadly no more having been lost many years ago due to quarry operations and the sinking of lime pits at Murrayshall. They lay just off the road there and consisted of bubbling springs with square stone blocks built around them. Entrance was by a wooden door. These springs may have been connected with the nearby Murray's Hall, or the original water supply for Stirling at Lessfeerie Springs, Touch. The term "boiling" would more likely refer to the movement of water rather than the temperature.

For over 400 years after Bannockburn in 1314, Cambusbarron's narrow path through time and the highway march of national history, follow different routes. Not until the Jacobite uprisings – the subject of another chapter – do they again converge, with the exception of 1651 when Cromwell's General Monck encamped his men briefly near the village.

From these intervening years only small fragments have filtered down to us. From surviving charters, for example, we know the names but little else of some of those whom at various times, included the village in their lands. In common with other parcels of land, Cambusbarron appears to have been constantly changing hands in feudal times from one greater or lesser magnate to another. In 1380 Adam More of Abercorn is the proprietor, but he later sells to one Hugo de Eglinton; in 1482 – 10 years before Columbus reached America – Matthew Forrester is part owner, along with Alexander Lamby of Drumberry, though by the early 16th century it is recorded that Cambusbarron was included in the property of "the Priory and Convent of Stirling"; Alexander Erskine of Conglour held the title deed in 1560, and by 1603, the land again belonged to the Forrester family., this time to Sir James Forrester of Garden; in 1635, to John Earl of Mar, and in 1672 David Moir of Leckie is in possession, but only for a short time, until he sold to William Leslie of Balquarn. (The name of an area of the village known until recent times as Leslie's Dryfields may originate here); and in 1682 the lands came into the ownership of William Wordie, about whom more is said later, and in whose family they remained until 1781 when they were divided up and sold as follows; 15 acres, called Kenning Knowes, to Alexander Buchanan; to Captain James Blair, Birkhill; to Alexander Blair, St. Thomas's Well; and an unnamed person bought the previously mentioned Leslie's Dryfields.

The exact dimensions and precise location of these "lands of Cambusbarroun", "land and mylne (mill) of Cammybarron", or "toun of Campisbarrone" as the area was variously called, is not recorded. Indeed, at the same time as these above-mentioned men were designated owners "of Cambusbarron", we also find recorded others who also "possesst lands *in* Cambusbarron". The prepositional change may suggest the major land owner was described as "of Cambusbarron" the "in" referring to the proprietor of a small area within the village.

If Robert Bruce is Cambusbarron's most noble visitor, it is probable that he was only one of several as, for many years during the reigns of King William and David, the village lay in the royal forest, or "King's Park" of Stirling. In his novel *The Black Douglas*, Nigel Tranter has his hero hunt boar in the lands of Cambusbarron before his treacherous murder by his king, James. Nearer our own times, in the final decade of the 19th century, the Prince of Wales, later Edward VII, was an occasional guest of the Murrays at Polmaise Castle, where he enjoyed the shooting. However, the most romantic of Cambusbarron's royal visits occurred in the momentous year 1745.

1 The boundary between Cambusbarron and its neighbour Torbrex, was marked for long time by a huge stone which lay at the side of the road between the villages. It disappeared when the road improved.

~4~

CAMBUSBARRON AND THE JACOBITES.

Until the construction of the Dumbarton Road in the early years of last century, the important military road that linked the two great castles of Stirling and Dumbarton passed through Cambusbarron. The village was a welcome staging post for travellers, and an old account refers to the warmth of hospitality accorded to both men and horses.

To any military force of the past, the strategic value of this road was considerable for, linking as it did the Fords of Frew, a few miles west of Stirling, it offered an alternative – possibly the only alternative – means of crossing the Forth, to that of Stirling Bridge.

Thus it was used on 13 September, 1745, by Charles Edward Stuart, the Young Pretender, as he travelled south from Glenfinnan with his small Highland force in the final, most ambitious and most tragic Jacobite Rebellion when Stirling Castle and Stirling Bridge were in the hands of Government troops. That night the Highlanders camped on the estate of Touch, for long a Jacobite house. (Though at this time Elizabeth Seton, the owner of Touch, was conveniently out of the district: a happy coincidence for the Seton family who, after Culloden, retained their estate, unlike those of other Jacobite families whose property was forfeited.). The Prince in fact slept that night in Touch House in a room on the north side of the mansion. (Until 1928 this retained some mementoes of his stay, including bedsheets and counterpane. And in 1946 Christie's of London offered for sale a gold ring presented by Charles to his hosts, and a maplewood quaich which the Prince used for drinking while at Touch.).

Dougal Graham, a poet-chronicler of the Rising (and one who may well have been a formative influence on the verse of William McGonagall) confirms the events of September 13–14 in his *History of the Rebellion*:

> "In the Moor of Touch that night they lay
> And some in villages nearby
> To Stirling then they marched down
> And through that place Cambusbarron town."

Before doing so, however, there occurred an incident at Touch, which, despite its historical insignificance, offers in its combination of pettiness, pride and tragedy, a wry comment on the whole sorry Jacobite affair. A Highlander, anxious to be fed, stole and killed a sheep belonging to one of the tenants of Touch, an elderly widow who, understandably, complained vociferously, the story finally reaching the ears of the Prince. A heated argument then arose between Cameron of Lochiel and the Chief of the Clan McGregor, as to the clan of the miscreant, with Cameron vehemently denying the popular belief that the culprit *was* one of his men. When that unfortunate was produced and was found to be indeed a Cameron, Lochiel's injured pride overbrimmed and in a fit of rage he shot the man on the spot.

When the poor victim eventually died the following day he was buried at the side of Old Touch Bridge (i.e. *behind* Touch House) and the spot was for many years called "The Highlander's Grave". The estate joiner, incidentally, being a staunch Hanoverian, refused to provide a coffin for the deceased, this being done by another joiner named Mellies, at one time a well-known name in the village (our last blacksmith was so called). When Elizabeth Seton returned and heard the story the estate joiner was summarily dismissed, his job being taken by his more compassionate fellow.

Meanwhile the Jacobites had left Touch and passed through Cambusbarron towards Edinburgh and victory at Prestonpans one week later. Stirling, its castle loyal to the government, was considered as yet too strong a challenge and was by-passed, though one story has it that cannon fire was exchanged when McLaren of Invernenty, eager to test the one Jacobite cannon of which he had charge, advanced from the safety of Cambusbarron (which was out of range of the Castle guns) on to the Kings Park. Two rounded pieces of metal dug up last century in Drummond's Nursery, which at that time extended as far as the Kings Park wall at Park Place, may be the cannon balls fired from Stirling Castle.

While this was taking place the Prince dallied briefly in the village when the then chief landowner and enthusiastic Jacobite, John Wordie, stopped the entourage and begged Charles to accept his hospitality. Displaying his characteristic charm, and lack of urgency which was to be a factor in the failure of his campaign, the Prince consented and refreshments were enjoyed in Wordie's home, Cambusbarron House.

This was not such a magnificent building as its title suggests, being a two-storey building some 40 ft. by 18 ft. which sat on the west of Cambusbarron Brae on a site until recently occupied by Cromwell Dairy. (The house was sold by Wordie in 1781 to John Graham of Cambusdrennie who resold it in 1786 to the bearer of a name well known in the recent past of Cambusbarron, one John Donaldson, described as a portioner or small land owner. Thereafter the building became ruinous and was eventually bought by Dr. Muschett of Birkhill around 1870 when it was demolished to make way for the new dairy).

Elizabeth Seton's more discreet support for the Jacobites in the '45 shows that she and her newly acquired husband Hugh Smith (they were in fact married at Linlithgow on 21 September, 1745, the day of the Jacobite victory at Prestonpans, he, as was sometimes the custom, altering *his* name to that of the Touch heiress), had learned a lesson from her father, Archibald Seton, whose part in the abortive 1708 Rising had almost cost him his life. Arrested and tried

for treason at the High Court in Edinburgh, Seton, along with several other Jacobite loyalists, was astonishingly acquitted after the trial had been grossly mishandled by the Lord Advocate. Understandably, Archibald was again suspect in the 1745 Rebellion when he was fined £500 for failing to answer a High Court summons – which he couldn't because he was out "under arms" with his kinsman, the Earl of Winton. When this rebellion was crushed, Archibald fled to exile.

Even after the disastrous conclusion to the '45, some local sympathy for the Stuart cause lingered on[1]. The political leanings of Cambusbarron's Jacobite families – the Setons, the Wordies and the Wilsones of Murrayshall – were all mentioned during the infamous trial in 1752 of James of the Glen, a visitor to all these local families, who was convicted and condemned by a Campbell jury for the murder of a Campbell. Stevenson incorporated James's tragedy in his "Kidnapped". And for many years after the Stuart cause had become a tawdry, if still romantic memory, the "Jacobite Ladies of Murrayshall" maintained a staunchly Jacobite household on the south side of Gillies Hill.; the Setons of Touch, like many Jacobites subjected in the years after 1745 to the indignity of toasting the King – to them the usurper King George – would gladly do so, but always discreetly drawing their glass over the nearest jug of water on the table to signify that it was "the King o'er the water" to whom homage was being paid, not the one in London. It was at Touch house in 1776 that there was danced what was to become a famous Jacobite reel by three nonagenarian Jacobites: Sir Hugh Paterson of Bannockburn and his sister Elizabeth Paterson and Katherine, Lady Barrowfield. The reel, robustly danced by the three old people was a final local gesture to a cause long since lost.

1   This despite the Jacobite's blowing up of St. Ninians Church as they retreated in January, 1746. The Church had been used to store gunpowder, and there is some doubt whether its destruction was deliberate or not. Several villagers killed, and the now isolated clock tower which amazingly survived the blast, stands as a memorial to an unhappy piece of historical vandalism.

~5~

FOUR LOCAL FAMILIES AND THEIR HOUSES

The Setons and their predecessors at Touch, the Frasers, had long been loyal to the Stuart cause. And they paid a high price for their loyalty: imprisonment in Stirling Castle, the Tolbooth and Newgate; heavy fines, exile and escape; death at Dupplin and Flodden.

Their property, the estate of Touch, was originally Crown land and the first mention of the family's ownership is in the 13th century when Sir Bernard Fraser, Sheriff of Stirling in 1234 is designated as being of Touch Fraser. Sir Bernard's descendants included the patriot Sir Simon Fraser who because of his loyalty to Wallace and Bruce – in whose guerilla campaigns he fought valiantly and selflessly – was eventually captured and executed in London by Edward I: Sir Andrew, Sir Simon (another) and Sir James – all killed at Halidon Hill in 1333, Sir Simon having distinguished himself at Bannockburn nineteen years earlier; Sir Alexander Fraser, brother-in-law to Bruce, and killed at Dupplin in 1332.

How the Setons came to possess Touch is unclear. Sir Alexander Seton, great grandson of the late Fraser heiress, Margaret, seems to have been the first of that name connected with the estate.

The only part of the present building that Sir Alexander would have known is Touch Tower, the oldest part of Touch House, which is said to date from the early 14th century. The present fine south facade of the house was built in 1747 by Elizabeth Seton and her husband Hugh Smith (who took the surname Seton), who reputedly engaged William and John Adam of the famous architect family. This was a time of improvement and confidence at Touch [1]: Hugh Seton had ambitions to be a great "improver" of the land.

He farmed on what was then considered to be a grand scale, his most important achievement being the draining of the carselands of the estate and the removal from them of peat, turning boggy ground of no value into high quality agricultural land. To this end he attracted Highland crofters to Touch whom he provided with rent-free farms on condition that they cut off the peat surface and cultivate the land below. By such policies the value of Touch Estate rose quickly from £500 to £2,000 per annum. Such prosperity did not last. After the death of his wife in 1775, the fortunes of Hugh Seton and his family went into decline. A combination of wild borrowing and extravagant living led him to the debtors' jail and exile from Touch. (Among the interesting attempts to gain capital to save the estate was an appeal to the Crown for back-payment of salary that was once, apparently, paid to the Laird of Touch for his services as Hereditary Armour Bearer to the Kings of Scotland. Shakespeare's villain-king Macbeth calls on Seton to get him his armour as retribution approaches. The appeal – for £12, 000 – was not successful)[2].

The final stage of Hugh Seton's life, however, was by any standards, an extraordinary one. From 1789, when he must already have been a fairly elderly man, until his death at Alexandria in 1795, he travelled, often on foot and in the appropriate native dress, through Europe, North Africa, the Middle East and India. And always, despite his eccentric life-style and past reputation, he was made welcome by the social elite in whichever port he entered. "Hugh Seton the Traveller" he was everywhere called. It was a title well earned.

If Hugh Seton was the most colourful of his

family, his son Archibald was the unsung hero. Forced to leave Touch at an early age, he spent almost all his life in the East, in the diplomatic service and after a lifetime devoted to repaying his father's enormous debts – over £45,000 – Archibald's diligence, selflessness and resourcefulness succeeded, and Touch Estate was redeemed. Tragically, Archibald's second ambition was never realised; returning at last to Scotland and the old house he had worked so hard for, this old bachelor whom his family in Scotland seem to have taken so much for granted took ill and died at sea on 18th April 1818.

The Estate passed to Archibald's sister Lilias, and then to a niece, Elizabeth Steuart of Allanton, and the family surname changed to Seton-Steuart. Thereafter Touch passed from childless brother to childless brother or nephew till 1928 when the incumbent, Sir Douglas Seton-Steuart sold it to Mr. C. A. Buchanan, whose family continue to live there. The house was used during the last war as a military hospital, and then as a civilian convalescent home, until 1959 when the Buchanan family again took up residence there.

The ordinary, often unnamed people of Touch are worthy of a passing mention in this narrative. They are also part of the historical fabric of Cambusbarron. Fergusons, Millers, Melles's, Johnstones, Stevensons, Neilsons, (one James Neilsons tenant of Bankend, appears before the Barony Court of Touchadam on 23rd July 1724 accused by his neighbour Humphrey Ure,[3] Kepmad, of assault) and Cowanes (the family of John Cowane, Stirling's most famous benefactor) were all prominent on the estate during the 16th, 17th and 18th centuries.

That the area once sustained a considerable community [4] is suggested by the many place names redolent of human life and activity that have been passed down to us: Dow's Craig, Gibbie's Steps, Gilmour's Linn, Mill Linn, Liddle's Craig, Brock's Craig are just a few. Sadly they tend now to be place names only, time having largely erased the distinctive feature that gave each place its name. Sometimes only a rickle of ancient, silent stones is all that remains.

One place name we do know the story of, however: Craigmarket on the road to Craignese Croft, derived its name from its use as a country market place during one of the plagues that periodically struck Stirling. Understandably reluctant to enter the town because of the risk of infection, but equally concerned about the loss of a valued source of income, Touch farmers and crofters organized a market near Craignese. Here they set up a cauldron of boiling water into which the people of Stirling, using a wooden ladle, placed their coins before retreating to what they considered a safe distance. The farmers would then advance, collect the money, and leave their goods to be uplifted in turn. This primitive form of protection was not entirely successful as several crofters caught the disease and died. A further precaution was the erection of a hut where anyone thought to be infected was confined sometimes for weeks at a time.

The victims of the plague were buried in the Chapel Park at the north side of Touch Garden. The Chapel, supposedly sited at the western end of the Garden near its boundary wall with the old road seems to have vanished a long time ago.

Another disaster to strike Touch in the 18th century occurred when the area was inundated by a water spout. Many houses and bridges were destroyed, and several lives were lost.

"Touch" itself means a hill and is one of the oldest place names in our area. Indeed there have been – or more strictly there continue to be – four "Touchs". Firstly there is Touchmollar, or "Touchmaller" as it was known in the 12th Century. This area lies immediately to the south and south west of Touch House and was originally owned by the Murray family but was sold in the late 15th Century to Sir Alexander Seton of Touchfraser (to the north and west of Touch House) which takes its name from its original owners.

The "maller" may derive from the Gaelic word "malair" meaning a merchant or a renter. Touchmaller and Touchfraser were combined to form, more or less, the present Touch Estate.

"Touchgorme" ("gorm" is the Gaelic word meaning "green") was the name given to the land that lay to the south and south east of Touchmaller – which we now refer to as North and Middle Third, and soon became part of the Barony of Sauchie; it is today absorbed into Sauchieburn Estate. The fourth "Touch" is that of Touchadam, (perhaps Adam's share of an estate, or possibly a corruption of the old Gaelic word meaning "the hill of the ox"), a title that refers to much of the land immediately around

Cambusbarron – the Gillies Hill Murrayshall, Gartur and Hillhead are included in it – and stretching away to the east of the village as far as Borestone at St. Ninians. This estate was owned for almost six centuries (until 1956) by the Murray family.

That this older title of "Touchadam" has all but disappeared is due almost wholly to the imposition on Cambusbarron of the name "Polmaise" by Colonel John Murray in 1865 to describe his new mansion in the woods above Cambusbarron "Polmaise" more accurately refers to the site of the Murray's former home, down on the Forth near Fallin. It is a pity that this more appropriate and venerable name has been lost.

It is not surprising that the Wilsones of Murrayshall were Jacobites. The family had come to Scotland from Denmark in 1590 with their mistress who was to marry James VI and become Queen Ann.

Their connection with Murrayshall dates from 1749 when William Wilsone, an Edinburgh lawyer then seeking refuge from the harsh political spotlight of the capital and the financial depredations caused by his allegiance to the house of Stuart – he had refused the oath of loyalty to the Hannovarian throne – occupied the mansion and became factor [5] to the Laird of Touchadam and Polmaise.

Murrayshall had been built in 1673 by the then Laird of Touchadam, the thirteenth, as a residence for his newly wed son and heir, John. It must have been a most attractive place in which to live, with its large mature garden, sheltered at the back by the cliffs of Gillies Hill, with a lily-covered pond at their base and fine views: to the south the Swallowhaugh Glen and the meandering Bannockburn; to the west, Touchadam Muir, Touch House and perhaps the modest towers of Touchadam Castle, the Murray's first home in this area; and the north-west, with its distant mountains. Here in the two-storey and garret house were born fourteen of John Murray's sixteen children, including two future Lairds of Touchadam. But with the building in 1697 of the new mansion house down on the Forth, its first family left Murrayshall. From whom William Wilsone acquired the house is unknown, but it seems likely to have been one

of the Murrays who occupied it until after 1697, possibly the heir(s) of James Murray who lived there until his death in 1743. Apart from his political beliefs which appear to have cost him much, little else is known about William Wilsone or his wife Lillias Haldane – one of the Haldanes of Lanrick, a family which also suffered badly after the Forty Five. Their family, though – eight sons and five daughters: Murrayshall appears to have teemed with children – certainly made their mark on the world, becoming successful colonists, doctors, bankers and merchants. Best known, however, were three who remained at Murrayshall all their lives, the maiden sisters Marion, Jenny and Lillias who became known locally – and then much farther afield – as "The Jacobite ladies of Murrayshall".

All three lived on into honourable old age and died in the old house under the Gillies Hill – Miss Jenny, aged 75, in 1823, Miss Marion, aged 85, in 1829, and her sister, Miss Lillias, aged 92, the same year; and to the hundreds of young relatives who visited them over the years, they bequeathed their store of Jacobite tales, legend and song. Every family meal for long ended with a toast "to Him over the water" and a contemporary account says,

> "There were two or three old ladies, Jacobites to the hearts core, who long after regular Episcopal Church was built, (previously the sisters would worship Torbex's Episcopal Chapel) continued as often as the (Hanovarian) royal family was prayed for, to shut their books with a slam, rise from their knees and yawn audibly."

Another writer comments:

> "Well do I remember the day on which the name of George was mentioned in the Morning Service for the first time; such a blowing of noses, such significant hums, such half-suppressed sighs, such smothering groans, and universal confusion can hardly be conceived."

"The Jacobite Ladies of Murrayshall", were, however no narrow-minded religious or political zealots and their home and its occupants became legendary for their universal kindness and hospitality, their house seldom being without guests, whether high – Bishop Gleig, the churchman was a regular visitor – or humble, perhaps the sick son of a local ploughman, to be nursed through illness, and every Christmas local cottagers and the like were made members of the Murrayshall community. With the death of Miss Lillias on 3 March 1829, the time of the Wilsones at Murrayshall was over. A great displenishing sale took place and most of the furnishings, ornaments and farm implements, many of them already antiques at the time, were sold. Murrayshall then became an ordinary farmhouse, losing much of its former grandeur when in 1866 the upper sections, considerably dilapidated, were removed. The then Murrayshall Farm [6] was eventually destroyed by the 20th century quarry operations.

The family Wordie was prominent one in Cambusbarron in the 17th and 18th centuries. Reference has already been made to Bonnie Prince Charlie's visit to John Wordie's Cambusbarron House in 1745 and the whole family was for many years committed to the Jacobite cause. The same John Wordie and his heir also John, appear to have given considerable financial aid to various families down on their luck because of their loyalty to the Stuarts – to the extent of almost ruining the family fortune: in the early 1780's the younger Wordie's financial affairs became so embarrassed that he drew up a trust deed in favour of his creditors and went off to Calcutta in an attempt to retrieve his position. He died there however, in 1787.

His grandfather, yet another John Wordie, seems also to have allowed his Jacobite heart to rule his financial head for his will, dated 1716, tells that his neighbour, Sir Hugh Paterson of Bannockburn, owed him 1,000 marks on nine years interest. A bad debt, as Sir Hugh lost all his possessions after the 1715 rising.

This John Wordie, already the owner of much of Torbex, obtained his Cambusbarron land in 1682, the same year he built Williamfield House. This can still be seen today, in Berkley Street, St. Ninians. Wordie also built Torbex, sometime later in 1721, which survives today as Torbrex Inn. Cambusbarron House was probably built around the same time, or perhaps as early as 1682[7] also, and Wordie may have intended the three houses to be tenanted by various members of his family who perhaps would have helped

administer his enlarged properties.

However, while Williamfield continued to be a home for some of the family in the 18th century – in 1759 a James Wordie is still living there – Cambusbarron was shortly taken over by John Wordie. Its history thereafter is outlined in an earlier chapter.

Torbrex House, meanwhile, was let to a John Buchanan, whose initials, those of his wife Elizabeth Campbell, and the lion rampant coat of arms of the Buchanan family, can still be seen on the outside wall of the Inn. Two letters "M.W." refer to the superior of the ground, Murray, (of Touchadam) and Wordie, the feuar.

In 1751, though, perhaps because of his increasing financial problems John Wordie sells off Torbrex House. Its roof for long afterwards offered shelter for many, including "Lady" Katherine Barrowfield, a daughter of the Patersons of Bannockburn, who cleverly effected the escape of her husband John Walkinshaw of Barrowfield from Stirling Castle, and a probable death sentence, after the failed 1715 rebellion. She was also one of the three nonagenarians who took part in the famous Jacobite reel at Touch House in 1776. Her daughter achieved even greater renown when she became the consort, and possibly the wife of an exiled Charles Edward Stuart. Their romance had blossomed at Bannockburn House in January 1746 when the Jacobite dream was fading, and Charles was retreating North.

Eventually becoming part of the Murray possessions, the fortunes of Torbrex House, like that of its owners, declined considerably in the 20th century until it was little more than a ruin. It was however rescued from total decay in 1970 and converted to an attractive inn. Less fortunate in this respect was Torbrex Farm, another Wordie property that was of some interest. The remains of the farm – it had been a ruin for a long time – finally disappeared when first the High School of Stirling, and then a large housing development were built in the early 1960's. It was occupied in 1771 by Isobel Wordie from Cambusbarron and her new husband Alexander Murray, grandson of the fourteenth Laird of Touchadam. Its most famous visitor, however, was the young Walter Scott, brought there on holiday by his mother in an attempt to improve his health. The house was at this time tenanted by Patrick Spark, a friend of

Scott's father, and it was from Torbrex that the young man travelled, in his host's carriage, on his first visit to the Trossachs, an area he was to make famous in his writings. Moreover, the future author's imagination must have responded to the rich historical associations of his holiday surroundings. His literary imagination was already quickened: Scott's hosts, the Spark family, treasured for many years afterwards, a descriptive poem he wrote during a ferocious thunderstorm over Torbex. The young Scott would also have known the nearby Episcopal Chapel of Torbrex which lay some 50 yards from the farmhouse, in the direction of Laurelhill. To here each Sunday would probably have come the Wilsones of Murrayshall and some other Stuart families to listen to the sermons of the Rev. Ninian Niving (died 1768) and his successor, the Rev. George Cheyne. All remnants of this small church have been totally erased.

Before acquiring their Torbrex Cambusbarron lands and consolidating them by their three houses, the Wordies lived in St. Ninians. The initials of a Thomas Wordie and his wife, the date, 1603, and the family motto, "Qui patitur vincit" – more succinctly rendered in Scots as "Wha Tholes Overcomes" once decorated a lintel in that village, and the interest from a sum of money, £1120, left by a William Wordie, was distributed annually to the deserving poor of the parish by the minister. By 1676 we find that the family star has risen sufficiently for (another?) John Wordie to be Sheriff Depute and Commissary Clerk to Stirlingshire. After 1780, however, that same star, at least as far as Cambusbarron is concerned, is in decline, and the Wordies fall from local prominence. Representatives of the family, nevertheless continued to grace its name with distinction, the most notable, perhaps being the geographer Sir James Mann Wordie, Master of St. John's College, Cambridge, and Chief Scientific Officer to Shackleton's 1914 Antarctic Expedition.

If the Wordie star sparkled brightly but briefly, that of the Murray family of Touchadam and Polmaise shone long and clear over the centuries. And when in 1865 Colonel John

Polmaise Castle, looking north.

Murray [8] took possession of his new mansion house, Polmaise Castle, in the Fir Park above Cambusbarron, the future and continued supremacy of the Murrays must have seemed assured. For in its combination of towers and turrets, crenellated battlements and balconies and its setting amongst pine woods, lakes and ornamental gardens, it must have symbolised for the Laird the strength, splendour, wealth and antiquity of his line. Yet it was all to end.

Such a thought could surely not have struck John Murray. This laird of Touchadam and Polmaise was the 22nd of his line, a representative of a family which had distinguished itself throughout the history of his country. His family had come to Scotland, possibly from Holland during the reign of David I. Then known as "de Moravia", they first settled extensively in the north-east of the country, in the area soon known as Morayshire. They were quickly engaged in the struggle for independence: Sir Andrew Moray, and his son, also Andrew suffering for their part in Wallace's campaigns, the former being imprisoned in the Tower of London, and the latter losing his life after Stirling Bridge in 1298.

The first of the family to be connected with our area was another Andrew, still termed "de Moravia" who in 1366 was granted "the lands of Kipmad" (still a local place name referring to the land *behind* – to the north – of Hillhead Farm). More significant is a charter by David II dated 28 August, 1369 granting Sir Andrew, "lands of Tulchadam and Tulchmolar". These lands, the charter records, were "to be halden blench of the King for Payt of one pennie".

The first Laird of Touchadam – note: not yet "Polmaise" – died in 1392 and was succeeded by his son William, still styled "de Moravia". The change to the simple "Murray" does not seem to have come until the time of the fifth Laird Alexander, in 1473. It is impossible to say which of the Murrays, Andrew or William or any later Laird, built Touchadam Castle, traditionally the first home of the family in this area. All that remains of it are a few clearly very old stones covered in grass and moss, but still decipherable as forming the foundation of walls, in the woodland – called "Morayeswood" in old maps – between Gartur and Murrayshall. A 19th century account described it thus:

"These foundations, unenclosed, nowhere exceed 2 ft. above the ground, are partially concealed by the growth of the turf, and all lie within an area of 90 ft. by 60 ft. The outline of an oblong building running east and west 42 ft. by 18 ft. and walls 3 ft. 4 ins. thick can be traced with two square buildings 15 ft. by 15 ft. possibly towers at each angle".

The area today is still referred to by its other venerable name of "Castlehill", or it is sometimes called "the haining shaw park" the phrase being an old Scots one meaning "enclosed woodland". Here, possibly till 1697 and the building of their then splendid new mansion at Polmaise, some at least of the Murrays possibly [9] lived (though the building a few fields distant of Murrayshall in 1673 for the Laird's eldest son (see earlier) perhaps suggests that this first and obviously modest building was by then proving less than adequate).

From the first, the Lairds of Touchadam showed themselves eager for power and influence, and the conflict that inevitably accompanies these. Sir Andrew himself became Sheriff of Stirlingshire in 1368. William, by judicious purchase, enlarged the estate. The fourth Laird, another William, became Honorary Armour-Bearer to James II before being killed in a quarrel in 1473 with a rival family the Bruces of Stenhouse.

(This seems to have been quite an argument as William's son James was also killed, and his heir Alexander may have died afterwards as a result of wounds received).

Clearly they did not heed the family motto: "Tout prest" – "Aye ready". An ancient document reveals that the King charged "Schir John of Carlisle to (bring) Lucas the Bruce and Douglas to the law for the slachter of William of Moravia etc.)"

The seventh Laird, Sir John Murray appears to have gained his title by kidnapping his predecessor and cousin David Murray and forcing him to resign in his favour. (This is recorded in a charter dated 3.9.1474). Sir John became Lord of the Council and twice served as Provost of Edinburgh. In between, ironical when it is remembered how he gained his title, we learn from another old charter that he was forced to surrender Touchadam to one Alexander Hume of that Ilk "against his will and for the salvation of his life". Sir John though, is knighted in 1494 by James IV.

William Murray, the eighth Laird regains Touchadam in 1508 after an appeal to the King who confirmed the estate as a "free barony". Less happily, though, William is one of the many to die at Flodden in 1513. His successor, John Murray, acquired forfeited lands in Lanarkshire before succumbing to the family failing of the time by meeting a violent end at the Battle of Pinkie Cleugh in 1547. In one sense, the tenth Laird William had the most profitable custodianship of all the Murrays, not only dying peacefully, but, through his marriage to Agnes, daughter and heiress of John Cunningham of Polmaise, added to Touchadam the extensive and valuable lands of that property. This aggrandisement continued with his son, Sir John, whose long tenure from 1569 to 1620 saw the estate grow further. Sir John served sixteen years as Provost of Stirling, was twice M.P. for Stirlingshire and was knighted by James VI, as was his son and heir William, who was also an M.P.

The thirteen Laird was another John and another Member of Parliament, but decidedly not a Parliamentarian, as he fought on the Royalist side during the English Civil War. For his loyalty to the Stuarts, John Murray, like many of his forefathers, suffered much loss, being taken prisoner after the Battle of Worcester in 1651, and having a £1,500 fine imposed on him by Cromwell. We should also remember this old Cavalier for his building of Murrayshall in 1673.

What was the attitude of his son, yet another John to the religious and political turmoil of the years of his tenure is unknown. Conscious of the physical and pecuniary wear suffered by his father and predecessors because of their involvement in national affairs, he was perhaps more circumspect. His one known contribution to the Revolution of 1688 when the Stuarts were finally exiled, was to take receipt for safe-keeping three silver cups belonging to St. Ninians Parish Church, who may have seen him as a figure of stability amongst turbulent events around them. It is possible also that the traditional ties of loyalty felt by the Murrays towards the Stuarts were then weakening. There appears little record of the family's involvement in the Jacobite years to come. Certainly in the 1708 affair, John Murray

was one of those suspected of complicity in the uprising and a warrant was issued for his arrest. But the comparative leniency of his treatment – while still technically a prisoner he was allowed to travel unaccompanied from Stirling to Edinburgh – suggests the government regarded his alleged participation as less than serious. By the time of the "Forty-Five", wherever the Murray sympathies lay, they did not voluntarily participate in the Rebellion, as is implied by an order issued to William Murray in January 1746 by William Comrie of Prince Charlie's army – once again in the district – to supply to Jacobites with meal, oats etc. "under pain of military execution". Another letter of the same time from John Murray, William Murray's nephew complains to the Laird that "if the present trubles (sic) be not soon at an end, it will put an intire (sic) stop to all Business". Not the sentiments of a rebel.

Perhaps John Murray preferred less serious conflicts such as that which became known as "The Battle of the Seats" when the rivalry that existed between Cambusbarron's two noble families, the Setons and the Murrays, spilled over into St. Ninians Parish Church. James Seton, it seems, became very jealous of an ornate Murray coat-of-arms which had been attached to the front of the Murray pews in the loft of the Kirk, and decided that the Seton insignia were also worthy of display. This he accomplished, but to do so was obliged to remove the Murray arms. This little fracas caused no end of bitterness, and was not resolved until it reached the Privy Council who ruled in favour of Murray.[10]

John Murray should also be remembered as the builder of Polmaise Mansion where he moved with his family in 1697. This was to be the Murray home for the next 168 years. And their move to Polmaise coincides with a less avid or overt involvement in the political affairs of their country. As Scotland moved through the martial confusion and complexity of Covenanting and Jacobite times into the relative calm of the Industrial Revolution and the age of agricultural improvement, so also do the Murrays appear to move from the sword [11] to the plough [12] and commerce. (Not always successfully, though: John Murray was one of those who invested in the disastrous Darien Scheme. His loss, £500).

Thus the future must have seemed one of

confidence and continuity to Colonel John Murray as he surveyed from the towers of his new castle in 1866 his ancient, extensive and prospering estate: some thirty farms, stretching from Hillhead and Kipmad in the west to Cowiehall in the south-east; three fine mansions – the new castle, Old Polmaise, near Fallin, and the beautiful Gartur House; and land rich in coal. His personal credentials were equally impressive. He had recently served with distinction in the Grenadier Guards in the Crimean War. His wife was the eldest daughter of the Duke of Montrose. He became friends with the Prince of Wales, the later Edward VII who visited Polmaise Castle to shoot on the Estate.[13] He performed all the duties of the genteel landowner, serving on many committees and boards. And indeed, when he died on 11 August, 1903 he had had a long, full and rich life. Yet one thing was missing: a son and heir.

One local tradition says that when Polmaise Castle was built in 1865, the site chosen was one much favoured by Cambusbarron people for picnics and walks, it having a spectacular view of the surrounding countryside. This spot was at its most popular in the autumn when locals would gather, often on what was called "Stookie Sunday" (Stook – the harvest sheaves drying in the fields) to admire the breath-taking sight and colours of the miles of fields whether ripe for harvest or freshly cut. (It should be remembered that most of today's built-up land would then be under cultivation). When the 1864–65 crowds were dispersed on the orders of the then factor, the story claims, [14] a curse of sterility was wished onto the Murrays by one angry villager, along with a prophesy that their new Castle would not last a hundred years.

This dramatic piece of local folk-lore is no doubt one that has gained in the telling, but it does point to a disturbing characteristic of the Murray line: of the last nine Lairds of Touchadam and Polmaise, only four produced heirs. John Murray did not. (Nor did three of his recent predecessors, which rather robs the curse of some force). John's successor in 1903 was his brother James, who too died without issue in 1907, and a brother again succeeded. Major Alistair Bruce Murray did have a son, but this young man was tragically killed during the opening weeks of the First World War, and with

him, at least as far as Cambusbarron was concerned, died the Murray line. His father, certainly, lived on until 1926, his mother for another thirty years afterwards till 1956, when on her death the heir, descending from a daughter of the last Laird, had the estate broken up and sold off.

A great two day displenishing sale was held in the Castle in April of that year. The catalogue described it as a sale of "Antique Furniture, Flemish Tapestries, Georgian Cabinet Bookcase, (sic) Oil Paintings, Silver Plate and Books", but this description does not do justice to the wealth of material on offer when over 1,000 items raised more than £10,000. Lot 3, for example, "an antique mahogany full size billiard table, 19 cues, rests, marking board, billiard and snooker balls, ball cabinet and three sets of rules" – £2.5/–; or the more genteel Cambusbarron housewife could have impressed her neighbours with Lot 117 which consisted of 17 deer heads and 6 sets of horns, all of which could be had for 5/–.

The sales catalogue provides an apt and perhaps poignant epitaph for a way of life whose time had passed. After 1956 the Castle, abandoned, vacant, gaunt and decaying, became an unofficial but endlessly fascinating playground for the children of Cambusbarron, who eagerly explored its long dark corridors, its cavernous rooms and draughty towers. The once luxurious but quickly overgrown gardens with their rhododendrons, groves, grottoes and lakes were also a source of adventure to local children, not to mention their parents. (It's a pity that numerous suggestions to turn the estate into a country park have never been taken up).

The condition of the ruined Castle deteriorated quickly until it became a source of danger to anyone entering it: floors gave way when stood upon, stairways crumbled and balconies crashed to the ground, and the final act came in June, 1966 when the Castle was blown up by the Army. Ironically, it outlived its curse by a single year, only to be razed to the ground.

The Murray name survives locally in many place names: Murray Place, Murray's Wood, Murrayshall, Murrayfield, but the power and privilege that held sway in this area for some 600 years is gone. Few will regret the passing of that power and privilege. This is the century of the Common Man. Yet there is also an undeniable sadness that such grandeur, such pride, such history, should vanish with such finality, and be represented today by no more than a heap of mouldering stone. McDiarmid might have been writing about smaller kingdoms when he said,

"Earth's littered wi' larochs O' Empires,
Muckle nations are dust.
Time'll meissle it awa', it seems,
An' smell nae must".

1　A late 18th century map of the estate held by Register House in Edinburgh is fascinating. Whether it depicts the estate as it then was, or represented future changes that did not, in fact, occur, is open to conjecture. It shows Touch House bordered on two sides, north and east, by a small loch fed by the Touchmoller (today the road that leads to Stirling's Waterworks) and parallels an estate entrance – a main entrance, according to the map – which begins just off the Touchmoller road at a point where today there is a gateway into a field. On each side of this entrance there is shown a lodge house, and from them, the avenue snakes through the field, crosses by bridge again, a narrow stretch of the loch and follows, approximately the line of the present avenue out onto the present Touch Road.

2　In October, 1901 Sir Alan Seaton-Stewart also made an appeal concerning his by then obsolete duties to the Court of Coronation Claims. Sir Alan's claim was not, however, for cash, but for official recognition of his title and permission to undertake his duties at the forthcoming coronation of Edward VII. He was no more successful than his 18th century ancestors.

3　The same Humphrey does not appear to have been a paragon of virtue himself: shortly after this incident, he is described by the factor of Touchadam as a "pretend tenant" and ordered to quit Kepmad.

4　See Chapter 1 for references to pre-historic relics in this area.

5　Wilsone was representing Murray interests as early as 1745. A letter dated 22nd September of that year – the day after Prestonpans – reflects the heady aftermath

of the battle: "All your relations are safe.... there has (sic) been such strange and amazing doings here for these last ten days that I cannot get to the country to attend your affairs".

6　A fragment of a local poem however, reveals something of the author's feelings for the house and its surrounding area.

The rugged road wi bend and turn
The Craigend Brig, the Limestane Burn
The dear auld hoose that sheltered me
The Slack, the Kilns, the Bunnet Tree.

D. McInnes

7　He is certainly described as living in the village by the following year.

8　The late Mr. James Morrison, who died in 1974 aged 95, recalls his first meeting with Colonel Murray: "A group of us, all laddies, about 15 or 16, were walking down the Polmaise Road one day when the Colonel came towards us on the other side. We all fell silent as we passed and looked away from him or down at our feet – we were feart! We were hardly past when he roared us back, and ordered us to salute whenever we met him anywhere.

We had to go back up the road, march back again, swivel our eyes right and salute! And we did it for years afterwards!".

9　Being landed gentry, the Murrays might also have one or more town houses in Stirling, and perhaps also in Edinburgh.

10　John's son, yet another John Murray, appears to have been equally disputatious: in 1705 – 1707 he became embroiled in litigation with the Town Council of Stirling, over his right to hold markets or fairs at Brocksbrae (near the Borestone) St. Ninians. The Council claimed exclusive entitlement to hold all markets within the immediate locality of the Burgh. Like the Murray and Seaton argument, this case went to the very top, with Murray displaying his considerable influence to have an act of Parliament (Scots of course) allowing him to hold two fairs a year. Stirling however, was not to be overcome so easily: after "a riot" (quote: Murray) instigated, it was alleged, by the Council had nevertheless failed to persuade Murray to call them off fairs. The Burgh magistrates decided that competition might work, and on the next Brocksbrae market-day organised a counter attraction – a series of races, some on foot, some on horseback, between Stirling and Cambusbarron. The road at this time passed through the Kings Park. A silver tankard inscribed "Stirling Pryse" was awarded to the winner of the horserace, stockings, shoes, gloves and a bonnet going to those successful runners. It worked; the Brocksbrae Market didn't and soon disappeared from the calendar.

11   This was not entirely true: for generations Murrays continued to make the army their profession – to fight not in Scotland itself, though, but against the King's enemies abroad. The last male of the line, Alistar Bruce Murray, was killed in France in 1914. One who did take up arms in Scotland, and who is of some interest locally, was the twentieth Laird, Major William Murray, who, as an officer in the Stirlingshire Yeomanry Cavalry took part in the suppression of the Bonnymuir Rising of 1820. An anonymous letter sent to Major Murray on 8th April, 1820 and "informing" on two Cambusbarron "radicals" reveals something of the flavour of that time when, for some, revolution seemed in the air. It is worth reproducing in full with original spelling and punctuation:

"Information for Major Murray" "That John and William Lamb, residing at the North End of Cambusbarron, have a military musket in their possession and was heard to say (just as John Downie, a private in the Stirling Troop was going to Stirling on Tuesday morning) that damn the cavalry for they could work the pike and gun they had better than the Kilsyth wavers (weavers?) and they were making up ball and cartridges for the battle and they would make Downie's blood run. This said in the presence of James Neilson, Cambusbarron.

I think that this should not be allowed to sleep. I dare not put my name here for my life but Neilson heard them say so and they were heard say this day that they were already for the cavalry now for they held plenty of cartridges made now".

The above mentioned Downie – perhaps he was the anonymous writer? – would have been a member of the government forces.

Several Cambusbarron men were in fact arrested in 1820 whether or not for actually taking part in the events at Bonnymuir, or merely on suspicion is not clear. On the day that the Bonnymuir Rising came to a savage conclusion when two of its leaders, Baird and Hardie, were executed in Stirling's Broad Street, Cambusbarron's radicals, several dozen, went into hiding in the surroundings countryside afraid of official surveillance and arrest.

12   A detailed breakdown of Touchadam and Polmaise Estate, along with tenants and their annual rents in the year 1772 may be of interest and can be found in the Appendix at the back of the book. The 18th Century spelling is retained.

13   One bird shot on the Estate in 1891 – not by the Prince – was an Osprey. It was latter stuffed and kept in the Castle.

14   There does seem to have been a degree of ill-feeling towards the Murrays at this time. And later in the 1880's and 1890's some disgruntled villagers complained that common land – especially on the Gillies Hill – was being walled off by Colonel Murray and added to his Estate. (Some walls were in fact cast down by angry villagers.) It is sad today that the only piece of Cambusbarron Commonty surviving is the "Free Green" at the junction of Quarry Road and Old Drove Road (or to give it its older name "The Commondry"). In bygone days village people could tether their animals here; fairs may have been held there; in later years it was a favourite spot for village bonfire. Today it is much eroded and diminished by quarry traffic.

~6~

SOME CAMBUSBARRON WORTHIES

Other less illustrious names than Bruce, Stuart, Murray and Seton have woven themselves into Cambusbarron's past and enlivened village life over the centuries. They, too, deserve their place here. The earliest record we have, and one of the fullest, is also one of the most interesting: William "Citizen" Jaffray who lived in the same house in Cambusbarron for the then very long lifetime of 78 years from 1750 to 1828. That he was a man much esteemed is evident from the following tribute which appeared in the *Stirling Journal* after his death.

"Benevolence beamed in his countenance and he seemed only in his proper element either when he was attempting to introduce something new, or when engaged in some active work of substantial kindness. When he died, he left a void in the country which has not yet been filled up, nor is likely to be filled up soon. For when will a man in his sphere arise, who will so disinterestedly confer such benefits upon society as the Citizen did?"

He earned the nickname "Citizen", of which he was very proud by his enthusiastic response to the French Revolution in 1789. Such enthusiasm did not find favour with the authorities, who, nervous about the spread of revolutionary fervour from across the Channel, issued a warrant for the Citizen's arrest. Fortunately for him he was away from home at the time; not so fortuitous for his brother whom the military took to be Jaffray and arrested, and who was incarcerated for some months, during which the Citizen, scorning discretion and prudence, visited him regularly in the Tolbooth with impunity.

His liberal philosophy is also evident in another risky episode he willingly involved himself in when a chance meeting with a negro slave passing through Scotland with her master, allowed the Citizen to translate his abolitionist sympathies into action. Having persuaded the negress that slavery had been abolished in Britain and that she need not be forced back to her destination, he and a friend helped her abscond from the canal boat on which they were travelling, and had her freedom officially acknowledged before a Glasgow magistrate.

William Jaffray was more locally revered, though, for his interest in another humanitarian cause: vaccination. Appalled by the number and the youth of those who fell victim to diseases such as smallpox, and impressed by the claims he had heard for inoculation, he refused to be deflected by his lack of medical knowledge and set about acquiring the information, skills and equipment he needed. Soon surgeries were held every Friday in his own house where the children of Cambusbarron, many of them the sons and daughters of his employees, for he was a weaver, would come for vaccination. On other days he would tramp the countryside to neighbouring villages and do the same work there – at his own expense – before beginning the return journey in the evening. (The town drummer of Doune was regularly summoned to announce the Citizen's arrival).

Thus was he able to estimate that by 1816 he had vaccinated over 13,000 children not one of whom he knew had ever caught smallpox. His attempt to eradicate the disease from his native Cambusbarron was temporarily impeded when two families living at opposite ends of the village refused "the jag" for their children. The Citizen's policy was however, sadly vindicated when deaths occurred in each household, while no other family was infected.

In his later years he received recognition for his work from the medical profession which presented him with a diploma and an inscribed silver cup – quite a tribute from an Establishment body to a man who had been regarded by authority for most of his life as something of a nuisance and potential troublemaker.

A final, more light-hearted memory of the Citizen: he was one of the first in Stirling to sport that new-fangled invention, the umbrella. Undeterred by public disapproval, he would walk in a stately fashion to church on a Sunday morning, carrying above his head what many of his fellow church-goers regarded as an ornamentation of vanity, an affront to the propriety of the Sabbath. It's doubtful is such criticism would have bothered William Jaffray.

The name "Grierson" is, or should be, one well known to the people of Cambusbarron. John Grierson, the pioneer of documentary film was not born in the village but came to it when he was two years old in 1900 and spent his childhood and adolescence here. He was always to remember Cambusbarron with affection, and once wrote:

> "Where I grew up you did not need to read it in the Bible: you just couldn't avoid lifting up your eyes to the hills. But what did I really have in my own bailwick to match their distant splendour? Yes I did have something: in its own special way the very mightiest of Scottish landmarks. I had the Gillies Hill, that one blessed knob of earth which settled the Battle of Bannockburn".

Cambusbarron even influenced one of Grierson's best films, *The Brave Don't Cry*. Forsyth Hardy, in his biography of the film maker writes:

> "The film was expressive of something central in his life. Since his boyhood in Cambusbarron the life of a mine had had a particular meaning for him. He had lived through grey days of depression and had seen his parents help to sustain a stricken community by running a soup kitchen. Now he had an opportunity to make a film which would present the miner's life".

Grierson's career in films and the world-wide reputation it brought reflects honour and distinction on his home village which was able to pay its own tribute on 10th October, 1967 when Dr. Grierson was asked to return to Cambusbarron and declare open our new primary school.

Of greater importance to Cambusbarron though was the film-maker's father, Robert Morrison Grierson who was headmaster in the village school for almost a quarter of a century, from 1900 to 1924. In many ways Robert Grierson fits our image of the traditional Scots village dominie, strong on discipline, and an advocate of the old values of hard work, decency, respect and orderliness. But he was for Cambusbarron much more than its schoolmaster. Perhaps his impact on the village can be summed up by this appreciation which appeared in the *Stirling Journal* after his death in 1928:

"In 1900 Mr. Grierson was appointed headmaster of Cambusbarron Public School. At the time the village was under a cloud, having scarcely recovered from the disaster following the collapse of the weaving industry at 'the mills". The school was a small one, but a revival soon set in, and in 1904, the school was practically rebuilt and largely extended. Mr. Grierson was a teacher with a high sense of duty to the pupils under his charge. Exceedingly painstaking and methodical, he took a keen personal interest in the children and did his utmost to stimulate and develop any talent they might possess. A disciplinarian with a stern code, Mr. Grierson was nevertheless well liked in the community, for his earnestness and concern for the welfare of his pupils were apparent to all. He was never "showy" in his work and never desirous of obtaining notoriety, but the excellent results produced at Cambusbarron School were frequently noted in the reports of H.M. Inspectors, while the number of his pupils who won bursaries in the various competitions open to the county or to larger areas was another tribute to the success of his labours. Mr. Grierson gave character building an important place in his scheme of instruction and the respect and esteem in which he was held in the village was demonstrated by the handsome presentations which he received from the inhabitants and former pupils in addition to other gifts from the staff and pupils of the school, and from the teachers in the St. Ninians district, when he entered into his retirement in the Autumn of 1924.

It was not only as a teacher, however, that Mr. Grierson was known to the people of the district. He interested himself in everything pertaining to the welfare of the community, being one of the original trustees of the Bowling Club, a pioneer in the movement to secure a public park for the village, and one of the leading workers in the War Memorial Monument. For a considerable number of years he acted as Registrar for the Cambusbarron district of St. Ninians Parish. A devoted churchman, Mr. Grierson held office for a long time as elder of St. Ninians Parish Church, and for several years he was superintendent of the Sunday School at St. Ninians. Possessing a strong personality he was kindly and thoughtful by nature and he left an impression on the life of Cambusbarron which will not readily fade".

He was in other words, one of the unsung heroes who work behind the scenes for the common good, usually taken for granted by the majority. Such people are the life-blood of any community and Robert Grierson was that to Cambusbarron. As the above hints, the closure of the Mill in 1896 delivered a sickening blow to the village: at one stroke over a thousand people were out of work; within one session the school roll fell by over a quarter; a "cloud" certainly did hang over every and any attempt to revive community life.

Many today should be grateful for his work. In recognition of the contribution and distinction brought to Cambusbarron life by both father and son, Stirling District Council in 1980 agreed to Cambusbarron Community Council's suggestion that a new housing scheme in the village be called "Grierson Crescent."

But Grierson was not the two-dimensional paragon the above perhaps suggests him to be. He was sometimes troubled by a deep pessimism when his liberal philosophy appeared inadequate against the events of his age. His son wrote of that philosophy:

"Behind it all was the dream of the nineteenth century – the false dream – that if only everyone had the individualist ideals that education taught, free men in a society, each in independent and educated judgement, would create a civilisation such as the world had never seen before. . .

The smashing of that idyllic viewpoint has been probably the greatest educational fact of our time. I saw the deep doubt creep into the mind of that schoolmaster that everything he stood for and strove for was somewhere wrong. What were the delights of literature when a distant judgement by a distant corporation could throw a man into six months of economic misery? What were the pleasures of Shakespeare and *A Midsummer Night's Dream* in the evening school, when industrial conditions were tiring boys to death? What was the use of saying a man's a man for a' that, when you were dealing day in and day out with a war of economic forces in which only armies counted and where motivating powers were abstract and unseen?"

Older villagers recall with affection, however, other human details that show a less troubled outlook: his nicknames – firstly "Auld Three Beards" because of the full goatee beard and very heavy eyebrows, and then, with advancing years, "Auld Bauldy"; his novel method of calming down excited classes –he'd march them round and round the playground until exhausted. His celebration of Cambusbarron School's record eight bursaries in the county examinations – the whole school was gathered in the playground, the results read out, and to the collective cheers the headmaster threw his hat high in the air eight times; his equally endearing habit of reading to the assembled school passages from *The Scotsman* on the latest wonder of the twentieth century, such as Bleriot's flight across the Channel; his provision along with his wife and eldest son, of a soup kitchen for the children of the unemployed; his broadening of the curriculum to include gardening and science – some former pupils remember the explosive experiments of "Professor" Wilson who stayed at Hayford House and offered chemistry lessons; his introduction, interesting when we consider the future career of his son, of film into the school as an educational aid; his teaching of Latin roots to eight year olds; his papers delivered to the local Popular Institute, on, for example, Carlyle and Ruskin; his doorstep arguments with the parents of the bright lads o' pairts, to give their son/daughter a chance and not to force them to work at fourteen.

One final memory of this impressive figure: from a 1919 photograph showing two

Veterans' Parade, 1919.

dozen survivors of the recent war, marching through Cambusbarron behind a pipe band, being cheered wildly; in the middle, almost marshalling the marchers as if they were once again his pupils, taking his place at their side, Robert Grierson.

James Henderson's claim to be regarded as a Cambusbarron character would appear to be invalidated by the lack of information we have on him. But he certainly made his mark on village life, being the only man known to have been burned in effigy here. This happened in the heady post-Reform days of the 1830's when Henderson, a weaver, made himself less than popular locally by publicly offering to go to London to swear that the property of several ardent reformers in the village was not of the requisite value to entitle them to vote at elections. Not only did the enraged radicals symbolically burn Henderson at Cambusbarron Cross in April 1837, but revealing feminist principles far ahead of their time, did the same for Mrs. Henderson a few days later.

Sadly, as with James Henderson, little information is left about village worthies of the past, save perhaps what their nicknames tell us. Who, for example, was "Pridefu' Jean" who behaved so much like Queen Victoria? Or "Sandy A' Thing" the pedlar, who visited the village to sell his wares in the company of "Hair-Oil Wullie" and "Shove Nell" a purveyor of black puddings?

Who were "Rocky" Campbell and "Blind Sandy" Shaw, and the unknown busker who tramped around the village playing a banjo, often being paid by the shopkeepers to go away? Or those unnamed [2] army veterans of the Crimea and Indian Mutiny who on pension days would appear in full regimental dress, and spend what one previous chronicler delicately termed "ambrosial nights in reminiscence"?

Of others we know a little more: our village blacksmith for many years after 1855 was John Melles, whose grandfather had shod Prince Charlie's horse at Gargunnock in 1745. The smithy of this time was at the house now called Sunnybank on the Stirling road. Mrs. Melles also helped at the forge, or provided tea and

Six Cambusbarron soldiers of World War I. Two, standing on the extreme right and left, had been wounded.

cakes for those members of the gentry who came to have their horses attended to. The eldest Melles daughter Margaret became at the age of twelve the under-maid at Dr. Muschet's Birkhill House, where she slept in a little trundle cot at the foot of the housekeeper's bed. She later became the village midwife. Tommy Hathaway was Cambusbarron's first taxi-driver, and had a hansom cab which transported villagers on important family occasions such as holidays. [3] Margaret Allan, a cleaner in the School before the First World War; known to the pupils as "The Duchess", she had read almost every volume in the Popular Institute Library, and was an influence on the young John Grierson, introducing him to writers like Byron and Carlyle. Alexander (Sandy) McLachlan whose energies in Victorian times diversified into weaving, tea-selling, Liberal politics, and verse; he is Cambusbarron' only known poet. Professor Henry Drummond who in the 1860's and 70's became one of the world's leading evangelists, began his career in the village where he and his father – of the Nursery family – organised a Sunday School. James Jackson J. P. who over fifty years till his death in 1940, was a good friend to Cambusbarron and a worker on behalf of the community; an enthusiastic reader, he donated many volumes and periodicals to the village library in the Popular Institute. And finally Dr. John Saunders Muschet who in the 19th century was a major landowner in Cambusbarron and lived in Birkhill House until his death in 1886. By profession a physician, Dr. Muschet also took an avid interest in the area. He was much involved in the prehistoric discoveries of Cambusbarron, many of them made on his land, and he claimed to know where other tombs lay, but chose not to reveal them. He was also behind early moves to build a second Cambusbarron Chapel, to be called "The Bruce Memorial". Dr. Muschet's rather eccentric brand of philanthropy had already been noted in his choice of architect for the proposed church; it emerges again in another of his pet schemes – an alternative Glasgow–Stirling railway line, running across the Fintry and Touch Hills and through the village which, the good doctor hoped, would sprout hotels, grow wealthy and benefit generally from the tourist and other passenger trade.

It may be that this catalogue of Cambusbarron worthies seems short and somewhat scanty, and lacking in the more modern village characters. Certainly many worthies, though deserving recognition have passed on without written note: they lived in a time when the tongue most emphatically prevailed over the pen, their deeds, traits, foibles and idiosyncrasies have gone unrecorded. Certainly also, the tradition of the village worthy continues, but he is better rendered when the perspective of hindsight has made for greater objectivity and discretion; and the passage of time lessens the likelihood of libel suits.

1 Mrs. Grierson seems to have been equally remarkable person devoting her energies to raising her family, teaching, the Suffragette movement and politics. In 1918, a time when women in Scotland did not on the whole take an active or public role in politics, she chaired election meetings for the Labour candidate in West Stirlingshire, Tom Johnstone.

2 See Chapter 8 for some names.

3 Our first village "Omnibus", ran in pre-1914 Saturdays to Stirling and back for 3d, and was powered by one horse driven by Tam Stewart. After the War the first regular bus service was provided by Sid Wyles. Consisting of a few seats and a platform for standing passengers, it cost 3/4d. for a single journey.

~7~

WORK

For Cambusbarron, as well as the rest of the country, the 19th century was time of considerable change. This was particularly so in the working life of the village where the traditional village crafts were overwhelmed by the impact of the Industrial Revolution.

By far and away the most common trade in the 18th and early 19th centuries was hand loom weaving, and time and time again in almost all surviving documents relating to village life in these times, one is struck by the prevalence of the weaver. For example, the Cambusbarron men who enlisted in the Loyal Stirling Volunteers against possible invasion by Napoleonic France in 1803 (war continued to touch Cambusbarron, however distantly) includes the following:–

John Aikman, Weaver, Cambusbarron, 3rd., or Captain Wallaces's; Charles Cowie, Shoemaker, Cambusbarron, 1st., or Captain Chrystal's; William Cowie, Shoemaker, Cambusbarron, 1st., or Captain Chrystal's; Robert Hosey, Weaver, Cambusbarron, 1st., or Captain Chrystal's; James Jaffray, Weaver, Cambusbarron, 2nd., or Captain Alexander's; John Leckie, Wright, Cambusbarron, 1st., or Captain Chrystal's; Peter McNiven, Weaver, Cambusbarron, 2nd., or Captain Alexander's; (The war had other effects: a diarist of the times notes how one George Moncrieff, an unemployed Cambusbarron "sawyer", hanged himself in Murray's Wood in April 1809. He could not get work "no wood being got out on account of the Baltic being closed against us").

Even as late as 1841, of the 236 Cambusbarron people listed in the census of that year as having employment, over 170 earned their living form the weaving industry [1]. Given that the Industrial Revolution was by this time well advanced, a surprisingly high number, 120, are described as hand loom weavers. Many of these continued to work as their predecessors had done independently of the larger manufacturers though *some* worked for a master who provided accommodation, looms and wages. "Citizen" Jaffray[2] was such a master, and in 1841 we find an Alexander Jaffray, perhaps his son, described as a woollen manufacturer:

These hand loom weavers mainly produced tartan cloths and when trade was good could earn 10/– to 12/– a week [3] but when bad only 7/6d. These wages were in sharp contrast to those earned in earlier more prosperous times. One weaver afterwards recalled:

> "Four days did the weaver work, for then four days a week as far as working went, and such a week to a skilful weaver brought forty shillings. Sunday, Monday and Tuesday were of course jubilee, lawn frills gorged freely from under the wrists of his fine blue, gilt buttoned coat. He dusted his head with white flour on Sunday, smirked and wore a cane. Walked in clean slippers on Monday; Tuesday heard him talk war bravado, quote Volney[4] and get drunk. Weaving commenced gradually on Wednesday".

But these palmy days were not to last and disappeared under a two-pronged assault: attracted by the high wages, other workers swelled the ranks of the weavers; as their numbers rose, so did the rates of pay fall. And gradually the hand loom began to yield to the power loom, as it did in Cambusbarron with establishment and growth of Hayford Mill.

Hayford Mill, or Cambusbarron Mill as it is sometimes called, was built on land feued from Cowane's Hospital in 1834 by three Cambusbarron men, John Campbell, William Watson and Alexander Donaldson, the latter two of whom previously owned spinning premises in the village. [5]

The building at this time occupied a much smaller area than it was to do so later, the first feu consisting of, in the original dimensions, 1 rood, 24 falls Scots (over $1/3$ of an acre), the second in 1837, of 3 roods, 14 falls, 2 ells Scots (just less than acre). But it was not until the 1840s, possibly 1845, when the Mill was acquired by Robert Smith and Sons that it flourished into a major business.

Robert Smith was already a prominent businessman when he became proprietor of Hayford Mill. In the 1820s he had been a wool spinner in Cowane Street; he then became the owner of the Old Bridge Mill in Stirling. He was also conspicuous in municipal affairs, becoming first a burgess guild brother of the town, then a baillie, and finally Dean of Guild in 1832. Under his influence, and that of his son, also Robert, Hayford Mill expanded to become, with the notable exception of Carron Iron Works, the largest factory in Stirlingshire, and at one stage the largest tweed manufactory under one roof in Scotland.

When Robert senior died in 1859, his estate included £2069 worth of machinery in the Mill stock worth £3,700 and Hayford House which he had built in 1850. His son continued the expansion, feuling yet more land in 1862 for additional building.

By 1869 at Hayford Mill, (or Hayford and Parkvale Mill as it was by then known) spinning and weaving winceys and other cotton and tweed materials, employed over 950 people,[6] who collectively earned approximately £19,000 p.a., producing goods with an annual value of £170,000. There were 530 power looms in the weaving section, and 13 sets of carding engines in the spinning department and all the machinery was driven by six steam engines with a combined 300 horse power. In 1871 the factory was further enlarged and over 1200 people were then employed. In 1875 the firm was sufficiently prosperous for Robert Smith to build the impressive mansion house of Brentham Park near Annfield.

There had, however, been some hiccups along this successful path of Victorian enterprise.

Hayford Mills. Notice Lime Road leading from the right-hand corner to Lime Mine in front of the Mill.

Interior of Hayford Mill.

In 1860, for example, the firm was in dispute with Stirling Town Council over the alleged pollution of the Forth, caused, claimed the town, by the dyes from the Mill being emptied into the nearby burn ("Raploch Burn", "Dirty Burn", "Mill Lead" and "Burnside" are all names that have been applied to this ancient stream; its oldest is best: "Glenmoray Burn") and thereby into the Forth at the Raploch, where, it was said, the salmon fishing was adversely affected. Of more concern was the effect on trade of the American Civil War during the early 1860's when supplies of cotton declined alarmingly, and in 1887 a serious fire destroyed part of the building. But most disastrous was the closure of the Mill in 1896.

Exactly why this highly successful enterprise collapsed is not clear. It is true that the textile industry nationally had been in decline since the 1860's but the failure of Hayford may have been more due to internal disharmony and mismanagement than to the vagaries of international trade. This was certainly the view of James Jackson [7] whose early career was spent at Hayford before moving to the Bridge of Allan firm of Robert Pullar and Sons, of which he eventually became director. Certainly something dramatic happened in October 1895 when Robert Smith abruptly left the area and moved (with his capital perhaps?) to London where he died five years later. A year after Smith's departure, Hayford and Parkvale Mills closed on October 19th, 1896.

The effect on Cambusbarron was profound. Hundreds of people were thrown out of work at a stroke. There was little alternative employment. While a pit had been sunk at Cowie in 1894, others at Fallin were not opened until 1904.

The three phases of reservoir [8] construction on Touch Estate for Stirling Waterworks had long since been completed; those at North Third and Earlshill were some ten years off. The increase in the village population, from 657 in 1841 to 1230 in 1881 – almost double in on generation – had largely been brought about by the attraction of the Mill as a source of employment. Within one year 1895 – 1896, the school roll in Cambusbarron dropped by a quarter, and even as late as 1904 – eight years after the closure – the number of parish electors in the village had climbed only as high as 299 in comparison with 336 in 1895.

Various attempts to revive the Mill were largely unsuccessful. During the First World War troops were billeted there by the Army. They practised manoeuvres on Touch Muir and used the field between the Mill and North End for drilling. Many were killed at the Dardanelles. After the War a carpet weaving firm occupied the premises; like other previous ventures this came to little, and the Mill eventually came into the ownership of the government who today under the auspices of the Scottish Home and Health Department use it as a storage depot.

Hayford Mill may not be the most beautiful building in our area (though attention to the unusual brickworks repays effort) but as a legacy of our industrial past, and as a major influence on the lives of our Victorian forefathers it retains an unusual impressiveness.

A song, sung by the female workers harks back to the heyday of the Mill, and is an endearing epitaph on that time:

"The servants think they're awfu' braw,
When they get a lilac goon or twa
A nice bit mutch cocked on their croon
But there's nothing beats a wincey goon!

They're aye sae neat, and aye sae sweet,
and aye sae trig and bonnie O'
Ah they could dance fornest the Queen
Cambusbarron bonnie lasses Oh!

An older Cambusbarron industry, and one that outlived the Mill by a few years is that of limestone working. (Here I am indebted to the researches of Dr. K. McKay published in *The Forth Naturalist and Historian*, Vo. 2, 1977).

The earliest recorded example of limestone quarrying in this area took place at Swallowhaugh in the small valley created by the Bannockburn before it now enters North Third Reservoir. From here, at the beginning of the 18th century, lime was extracted and transported

Troops billeted in Hayford Mill during World War I, preparing for Church Parade.

to Blairdrummond Estate for agricultural uses. Mounds of debris left by the quarrying can still be seen on the banks of the Bannockburn, as can the open horse-shoe shaped kilns used for burning the lime. Quarrying was also conducted, possibly from the same date, at the foot of Sauchie Crags, and a well-preserved kiln – a hollowed-out hole lined with boulders – excavated in 1971 can still be seen at M.R. 762 894.

Mining, as opposed to quarrying, was carried out at Craigend, (near the Limestone Burn) where mine entrances and kilns survive. At the end of the 18th century, 16 miners were employed here, and earned 10/– a week to produce about 1800 tons annually. By 1842 their wages had increased to 15/– a week, and 10/6 in the case of labourers. Mining was also the method of working at Murrayshall Lime Works, where again kilns and mine entrances survive. Owned by the Murrays of Touchadam, 12 men were employed here. By 1837 the annual production consisted of 1350 tons – which sold at 15/5 ($77^1/_2$p) a ton. The lime was worked from a mine which went 400 yards into the hillside.

The remains of Cambusbarron Lime Works can be seen today in the kilns at Hollandbush and the mine entrance in the field next to the football park and bordered by the Mill Road. When exactly working began at Cambusbarron is unclear, but the way was paved by William Murray of Touchadam who succeeded to the estate on the death of his father in 1814. Even before this in 1810, he had persuaded his father to allow him to "dig" for lime under the old and new Fir Parks, i.e. Gillies Hill. A mine entrance still visible in the middle of the Gillies Hill woods is possibly evidence of this enterprise, and remnants of saddles and harnesses found nearby suggest that the lime was transported by pack horse. (Before the First World War, it was possible for the young Alistair Murray to travel up the waterlogged entrance in a boat he had dragged from the lake on the Estate). The following year 1811, the younger Murray obtained two parcels of land he needed for his scheme costing £700, one, from George Callander of Craigforth, being that part of Hollandbush where the kilns were later built, and the other being the field nearer the village where the mine was sunk; this he received from John Graham of Gartur in exchange for that part of Touchadam

called Bankend. In a letter to his father in November of the same year, William looks forward to beginning working for lime, and ends his letter optimistically, claiming that while neither he nor his father would benefit much from the enterprise, in time the Estate [9] certainly would.

The mine burrowed in a south westerly direction under the Gillies Hill, meeting in air-shaft at Map reference 774 923, or more familiarly, immediately behind what was once called the Fairy Hill, just off Old Drove Road. This shaft is now filled in, but is still recognisable as an unusual hollow in the ground. From here the mine breaks up to form a network of tunnels and cross tunnels underneath the northern slope of the Gillies Hill, some stretching almost as far as Polmaise Castle. At the time of the mine's closure in 1909 between 20 and 30 men worked there, toiling from 7 am. till 3 pm. often having to stuff bunches of straw into their mouths as a relief from dust. Tools, which were re-sharpened daily , were collected from the smithy near the entrance to the mine – on the site now occupied by Forsyth's coal merchants: dynamite, which the men had to buy themselves, was obtained form the store-house halfway between the mine and the kilns. The extracted limestone was carried from the mine by a series of hutches, each of which would hold about 15 cwt. when full. They were drawn by rail to the kilns some 600 yards distant by an endless chain powered by a steam engine. After burning, the lime was carried $^3/_4$ mile by standard gauge railway line to meet the Old Forth and Clyde Junction Railway near Bankend Farm. The raised banking incidentally, on the western side of the football park, was constructed by the owners of the mine and used to be known as "The Lime Road". It was formerly regarded by villagers as a right of way, and many used it as a route to the Mill. One proprietor of the mine, a Mr. Johnstone, at one time occupied the house of East Hayfield where he stabled some of the mine horses. A villager who knew him described him as "a miser". . . (who had) "the leanest horses that ever walked on four legs". Boys used to chant after him in the street:

> "Johnstone's auld naigs,
> they're stuck on the Brae,
>   Wi fower pailin stabs,
>   and a wee puckle stray".

Another early 19th century industry, less durable than weaving or lime working, was distilling. This was carried out at Glenmoray Distillery in the Burnside area. (Glenmoray is the name for the small valley that the burn runs through; the large recently modernised building opposite Mill Road is called Glenmoray). It must have been a fairly modest concern, perhaps too modest as on January 20, 1820, it is advertised for public sale. Included in the transaction were:

"A large copper boiler; a small copper boiler; two copper stills with apparatus complete; a large mash tun; under bank copper pump; nine wash tuns; four coolers and sundry other articles of brewing utensils; also ten sacks of malt".

Six months later the business is again on offer, this time described as "commodiously situated for coal and receipt of grain and delivery of whisky within two miles of several coal hills and not $1^1/_2$ miles from the Stirling shore. Two stills of 600 gallons, etc. Sufficient supply of water at all seasons".

No trace of Glenmoray Distillery is apparent today, though some villagers will remember the building called "The Barns" which stood at the beginning of the Mill Road on what is now open grass. This, as its name suggests, was originally used for storing malt [10] for distilling.

Other Victorian industries gave employment to some Cambusbarron people.

Quarrying the stone from the Gillies Hill was carried on long before the present workings at Murrayshall and Cambusbarron; the remains of an old quarry can still be seen at Bearside, and old maps indicate the site of a quarry in the middle of what is now the Gillies Hill housing scheme. This may be the site from which in June 1743 one James Richardson was given permission by Polmaise to quarry building stone. A sawmill was in operation just inside the woods near the main entrance at Gillies Hill; a few dressed stones forming what was once a small well, or pool, now dried up may be connected with it. Reservoirs were constructed on Touch Estate to provide water for the town of Stirling. The first, in 1848, has since become the present waterworks. No. 2, built in the same year, holds 15,860,000 gallons; No. 3, constructed in 1864, holds 48,009,000 gallons; No. 4, completed in 1881 has capacity for 121,541,000 gallons. Sand was extracted from a pit next to Birkhill House, on land presently taken up by the motorway. Also in this area, Drummond's Coneypark Nursery, until the recent past, gave employment to Cambusbarron men for over 150 years.

1 Other trades included: domestic servants, farm labourers, shoemakers, wrights, and a 10 year old Sally Dick apparently earned her keep by being a "cowfeeder and herd".

2 A young William Jaffray was one of those Cambusbarron weavers who won a long drawn-out battle against the weavers of Stirling in the 1770's and 80's to be allowed access to the yarn market there at the same time as the town weavers. Previously entry to the market by the country weavers was strictly limited. Weavers from outlying areas contested the action. Other Cambusbarron men involved were James Kidston and John Watson.

3 Wages for other trades given in the 1793 Statistical amount were: shoemaker 14d a day; stockingmaker 1/–; tailor 10d. and victuals; carpenter 9/– a week; cart and plough-wright 8/– a week; mason 20d a day; blacksmith 9/– a week; tanner 1/3d. a day; malster 12 guineas and victuals per annum; man-servant £9 to £10 per annum and victuals; nailer 1/3d a day; wool comber 1/3d a day; maid gardener 1/2d a day; slater 2/3d a day; cooper 4/– a week and board; baker £11 per annum and board; sieve-wright 3/6d a week and board; clock maker 10/– a week; tanner 7/– to 9/– a week

4 Volney – a French political writer who celebrated the working class.

5 This building was in fact at the foot of the brae on the bank of ground now covered by grass and trees in front of the Social Club. Older villagers will recall it being referred to as the "Old Church", which indeed it became in the 1860's and remained so until the building of the present church is 1910. See Chapter 8 "The Social Scene".

6 Some of the younger workers were called "half-timers", spending half their day at work and half at school.

7 See Chapter 5 "Some Cambusbarron Worthies".

8 Stirling's water supply before 1848 came in pipes from Lessfearie Springs, also on Touch Estate, just to the west of Woodside Farm. This began 1774. In 1848, the now redundant Springs were diverted to help Cambusbarron with water. The 1848 scheme incidentally seems to have cost Stirling Town considerable effort not to mention money, as the plan was vigorously opposed by one Robert Henderson of Allanpark. The contractors eventually began work in September 1848 – after the harvest had been gathered – and piping was laid across Kepmad and Whitehouse Farms and then to Stirling. For further details see end of chapter.

9 Lime must also have been worked in earlier times by the tenants of Touchadam: a letter of July 1751 from Hugh Seton of Touch, to William Murray of Touchadam complains about the latter's tenants who, it was alleged, sold Seton short measures of lime. Murray neatly side stepped the complaint by informing Seton that while Touchadam tenants might take lime for their own use, they were forbidden to sell it, "Otherwise it will become exhausted".

10 Malt storing took place at St. Thomas Well.

~8~

THE SOCIAL SCENE

Villagers, passing the Church, may notice leaning against the outer wall of that building an old weathered stone slab. Still decipherable is the lettering which reveals "Cambusbarron Subscription Schoolhouse 1828". It is appropriate that school and church are seen to be linked, however symbolically today, since it was the Reformation, with its call for a school in every parish which gave impetus to widespread education in Scotland. By the time of the 1872 Education Act which for the first time made schooling compulsory, most parishes and almost all in the Lowlands, had maintained a school for a considerable time. But for many larger parishes, like that of St. Ninians in which Cambusbarron lay, one parochial school was inadequate and other kinds of school sprang up. Such was Cambusbarron Subscription Schoolhouse, a small two storey wooden building which until 1909 stood on the site now occupied by the Church. The lower storey was used as a classroom, the upper perhaps providing accommodation for the schoolmaster. The quality of education offered by these schools varied greatly; some could rival that of any burgh grammar school; others consisted of an old man or woman teaching what little he or she knew for a few coppers provided by parents. That Cambusbarron School was of this latter, inferior type in 1834 might have been the reason for the petition got up by the villagers in July that year, asking the local Kirk Session to supervise the conduct of the village schoolmaster, a Mr. Thomas. Exactly why Mr. Thomas's conduct required supervision is unfortunately not recorded, but the following year his place had been taken by a Mr. McDermaid.

By the 1860s this school which held up to 80 pupils had in turn become inadequate to the needs of the growing population of Cambusbarron. Its last master described it as "a miserable place", and in 1868 a Committee of Management was elected at a "meeting of the subscribers to the New School". It comprised Robert Smith, proprietor of Hayford Mills, as president, James Gray, secretary, Jas. Melrose, cashier at the Mill, Vice President, and D. McNaughton, grocer, treasurer. The trustees were Robert Smith, Sir Henry Seton-Steuart of Touch, Henry Drummond of Glen Elm and Col. Murray of Polmaise. The annual subscription was set at 1/3 except for committee who paid 2/6. Within a year, plans for altering the old schoolhouse were drawn up by a Mr. Mathieson, but the cost of such work, £900, did not find favour with the committee who imposed a £500 limit and declared that "the school room and teacher's residence were not according to instruction" and Mr. Mathieson was sent back to the drawing board. It did not matter. Events at a national level were over-taking village concern. In 1870 the Education Act was passed for England and Wales. The Scottish Act followed two years later. By 1875 Cambusbarron had its new school.

The school – now of course the Leisure Centre – was then much smaller than the present building, and at a cost of £4,000 accommodated in 1875 161 children and 2 teachers. This meant average classes-sizes of 80: those who look back to mythical golden age of Scottish education might consider such details. In addition, the teachers had two pupil monitors to help them – bright children who received instruction from staff, and then tried to pass that on to their fellow pupils.

The school enlarged to its present dimensions

in 1906–07 under the guidance of Robert Grierson. By then Cambusbarron was beginning to recover from the effects of the closure of the Mill; new pits had been opened up locally, principally in Cowie, and the village population was again rising. The extension included a new infant department of three rooms with accommodation for 160 pupils (again this meant a large pupil-teacher ratio of over 50 pupils per class) a central hall and separate cloakrooms for girls and boys. The new wing was built onto the back of the existing school i.e. only the entrance marked "Boys" and the two classrooms on either side formed the original building. Playsheds and lavatories were also added, as was a further half-acre of playground.

One of the earliest references to a teacher in the district is in 1653 when the Parish Schoolmaster, Mr. Alexander Cunningham, was summoned before the Kirk Session to answer certain questions; viz

> "that the said Mr. Alexander Cunningham did not wait upon his charges.[2] that he did stryk the bairnes wit his staff to the hazard of their lyfes.[3] that passionately did he curse the children. [4] that he did leave out of the rolls diverse names of children baptized".

The fortunate Mr. Cunningham was admonished with a warning, there being no firm evidence against him. He did not, however, remain long in his position thereafter; nor, indeed did many of his successors, and the Parish got through at least eight schoolmasters in twelve years. Whether it was the gimlet eye of the Kirk Session hovering over his schoolhouse that made the schoolmaster's job a short-term one, or whether it was the length of his working day, from 7 am. to 5 pm., is not made clear. Possibly it was more to do with that complaint of the Scottish dominie since even before Mr. Cunningham's day, his salary.

A memorial, drawn up in 1792 by parish teachers, expressed their discontent with their lot:

> "Ninety years have produced such a change and so great an improvement in agriculture, navigation, commerce, arts and riches of the country that £15 sterling per annum at the end of last century may be considered a better income than £45 at the present time. Suppose

then that in Scotland there are 900 parochial schoolmasters, which is near the truth, 800 of them will be found struggling with indigence, inferior in point of income to 800 day labourers in the best cultivated parts of the island and receiving one half of the enrolment of the menial servants of country gentlemen".

Certainly our local schoolmasters do not appear to have been generously remunerated. In 1793 – a year after the above mentioned memorial – the salary was £14 12/–, though the local minister also insisted that the incumbent enjoyed, "Other perquisites. . . besides an excellent dwelling house, school house and garden". Even by 1829 when salaries had been improved through Act of Parliament, the local heritors decided that the schoolmaster's salary, "Shall be equal to the average price of two chalders of oatmeal".

And to qualify for this wealth the parish dominie had a heavy workload and according to an 1809 advertisement the successful candidate was expected "to teach English, English Grammar, Latin, Greek, French, Writing, Arithmetic, Book-keeping, and practical Mathematics". In addition he was also to recruit and pay at his own expense, an assistant teacher. Both these fortunate souls would teach in a building erected usually at minimum expense to the heritor. A new parish schoolhouse built at St. Ninians in 1787 was described only 18 years later by the local minister as "incommodious and insufficient", and it was pulled to the ground and rebuilt.

Cambusbarron Public School's first head may have been George Bowman [1] who was certainly headmaster by 1881. In the same year, another George Bowman – perhaps a son – is also described as a teacher in Cambusbarron as is, in the following year, Mary Christie.

By August 1896, these latter two had departed and the complement of the school comprised, besides the head, Jane Dobbie, described as "headmistress" and two "assistants", Jane MacDonald and Cathie Wilson. The school roll was 221. Two years later an HMI report commented unfavourably on the school. It had "an impression of noise and bustle... registration should show fewer corrections".

Besides this official inspection, the school was visited regularly – as many as 16 times in a session – by members of the Parish School Board, to ensure it was being run in a disciplined and orderly fashion. There were, however, pleasant diversions from the rigours of school. On October 25th 1898, for example, the children received a half day thanks to the visit to the village of Peter McKay's Fair; Messrs. Barnum and Bailey's Shows in Stirling closed the school on 21st August 1899; and on 6th June 1900, the Chairman of the School Board, J. T. McLaren, (also factor at Polmaise) declared a holiday to celebrate the British Victory at Pretoria during the Boer War.

George Bowman vacated his headmastership under mysterious circumstances. On 29th May 1900, the School Log Book records "Master called urgently to Glasgow". The following day Bowman himself wrote "I have this day resigned the headmastership of this school". Soon afterwards he left for South Africa where he died some years later.

The Log Book entry of 14th August 1900, records that "Mr. G. Bowman having resigned, Mr. R. Grierson, the new head, began duties on this date". It is clear from the ensuring entries that Grierson was a new broom, discovering then righting weaknesses. Soon he had obtained much needed drill equipment, and even musical instruments. He completed his first day by declaring "In no respect can the work of the classes be said to be well advanced". Gradually though, the quality of education at Cambusbarron improved. It is interesting that the Log Book reveals that the children at this time had to attend school on Christmas Day. Continuation classes – night school – were held, those in dressmaking and joinery – the latter taken by T. Anderson, master of works at Polmaise – were very popular.

Soon however, the old school was too small to accommodate all the pupils. By 1905 some pupils were having to be taught in the nearby Popular Institute (the *former* schoolhouse) and the winter of 1906/7 saw the extension of the school buildings already referred to. The actual work caused problems: on 8 February 1907, Grierson complained in the School Log about the "interruption to work because of workmen". Other interruptions continued to improve the routine of school-life; on 21 March 1906, a half-day was given so that children could visit a "menagerie". Less happy were other visitations which affected the children's education: scarlet fever, whooping cough and the like were common diseases closing the school sometimes for weeks on end. Lessons were also briefly suspended on 9 December 1907, as a mark of respect for the Laird of Polmaise, James Murray, who had just died, and similarly on 20 May 1910, to mark the funeral of Edward VII. Indeed the Grierson household itself was not spared when in September 1906 the School Log revealed that the headmaster was absent attending the funeral of his daughter.

This was the time also that Grierson and his wife, concerned about the physical well-being of the pupils of the poor and unemployed, began their soup kitchen. He refers to these in the Log in 1909 and 1913, though former pupils recall them on many other occasions. Also recalled is the week-long holiday in 1911 to celebrate the coronation of George V.

The First World War came early to Cambusbarron and its first impact was on the School. The Log of 17 August 1914, states: "Owing to War, part of School premises have been taken possession of by Army Officers". Temporary accommodation for the senior class was found in the Parish Church Hall (now the Community Centre). The military surrendered – temporarily – part of the school in May 1915, when Grierson crustily remarks "Returned to School premises which were found in blacken-ed condition by the Military". However, the army intermittently occupied the School throughout the war and classes were taught in various buildings in the village. The end of the hostilities did not bring an end to illness. Once again, the Log of 1919 records the prevalence of scarlet fever, whooping cough, measles and mumps in the village.

Robert Grierson retired as headmaster on 30 August 1924. He was succeeded by Mr. David James, who was introduced to the school on 4 November 1924, by the Covenor of the School Board, Mr. Duncan Robertson, who, having done so, declared a half-day's holiday. The following month the children assembled to pay tribute to their old head, who was presented with various gifts. Just over four years later the school had one of its last unofficial – the tradition was fast disappearing – holidays for Robert Grierson's funeral. One "tradition", initiated by Grierson had evidently continued when during the General Strike of 1926, "the feeding of necessitous children" had taken place.

Another death, and one which shocked the School in the 1920's was that of Miss Hamilton, a popular and long serving teacher who died, on duty, on 29 October, 1925; the children lined the streets during the funeral, and a plaque to her memory in the old school testifies to the affection and esteem in which she was held.

This was also the time of other near legendary teachers whom many villagers remember, often with affection and respect, sometimes awe and fear: Miss Thomson, who joined Cambusbarron in 1915 and taught there for 43 years; Miss Anderson who served almost as long; Miss Guthrie, Miss Peacock, Miss Cameron. Mr. James was succeeded in 1938 by Mr. Peter Webster who saw the school through the difficult war years when, for part of the time, 62 evacuee children from the Glasgow area were billeted in Cambusbarron. The nearby B.B. hut – on the site of the present Church Hut, was used as an extension to the school, three classrooms being formed by judicious use of curtaining. The end of hostilities was celebrated with two days holiday on 8 and 9 May, 1945.

After the War the school was guided in the early fifties by Mr. J. N. K. Henderson, then by Mr. Matthew Goodwin, who handed over in 1965 to Mr. James Reid. Mr. Reid's term of office saw the move from the old to the new school in 1967. Mr. Reid's successor, Mr. Masson in turn handed over Mr. Bob Cook who retired in 1992.

When in 1870, plans to modernise and enlarge the old schoolhouse were abandoned, and the "new" school was built just to its east, Cambusbarron was left with an old but still potentially useful building. In January 1876, a public meeting called by a handbill was held in the new school to discuss how the village might best derive benefit from the building and its surrounding land. A suggestion that a bowling green be laid out on the land was vetoed by Col. Murray of Polmaise, who thought the area of land insufficient for such a purpose; moreover he wanted the schoolhouse retained. As the landowner, his words carried heaviest weight. A suggestion – deriving from whom it is not known – that the premises be converted into a Library and Reading Room found more favour, and Col. Murray began the Subscription List by donating £20: this was matched by Robert Smith of Hayford Mill, who also provided the library of the then defunct School of Art in Stirling. A committee, comprising Mr. Smith, Mr. Robert Taylor, Mr. Henry Stark. Mr. James Melrose and Mr. Andrew Milne, was formed to negotiate the details of the lease with Col. Murray.

The Colonel readily agreed to lease the ground for as long as the village wanted, at only a nominal rent, with one condition: "that tea, coffee etc. could be supplied to members, but no wines, beers or spirituous liquors". An interesting proviso: the present admirable village Social Club is directly descended from the old School House. Local tradesmen Donaldson, Chalmers and McGregor agreed to undertake the renovation work. Collectors requesting subscriptions visited every house in the village, and thus was born in January of 1877 not only a village library and reading room, but, to give it its full title, The Popular Institute. The adjective chosen reflected the hope of its founders that the enterprise would find favour with ordinary people of the village; it did not describe the frequency of attendance. The popularity of the Institute indeed varied considerably over the next ninety-odd years of its existence, but in its heyday it provided for the village not only pleasant and inexpensive recreational facilities, but also, especially in its early years, a refuge from overcrowded rooms and noisy families for villagers attempting to improve their education.

The first subscription in 1877 was 3/– p.a. or 1/– a quarter, or £3 for life. Books were issued only on a Monday evening from 7 to 8.30, the first half-hour being restricted for the exclusive use of ladies. Only one volume was allowed per person, unless half the subscription was paid again; there was a 1d a week fine for overdue books, and a fine of 1/– imposed on members who subsequently lent book to non-members. The first caretaker was a Mrs. Monks.

Gradually less intellectual distractions were added to the Institute's facilities. Bagatelle was obtained at $1/2$d a game and draughts were provided, and in front of the Institute, two quoiting or "kyting" rinks were laid out within a wicker fence which stretched out into the Main Street much farther than does the present boundary of the Church. Kyting involved throwing metal rings, or horseshoes and attempting to ring a metal rod hammered into the ground some distance away. Like bowls the winner was often the first to reach 21 (though sometimes games were not decided until the winner scored 60 shots) 2 shots being gained for a direct ring 1 shot for each kyte that was nearer the "jad" than your opponent's. At the Institute, a game cost 1d. It was very popular at this time often being the subject of inter-village competition and rivalry; sometimes large wagers depended on a player's skill. Cambusbarron's other kyting pitch was on the ground in the West End now occupied by the Council as a yard and lorry depot.

By 1886 the Institute had been renovated yet again and £50, raised by a series of concerts and recitals, was spent in trying to render it more attractive to villagers – a sign perhaps that its popularity had begun to wane. The money was spent buying over 200 new volumes, mainly histories and travel books; the Institute subscribed to various local and national newspapers and rooms were let to suitably respectable local groups such as the Y.M.C.A. The Cambusbarron Brass Band practised on summer evenings on a makeshift bandstand at the back of the Institute and a billiard table was purchased; (its introduction though led to rowdy behaviour from some members).

By 1891 the condition of the Institute needed further attention which was undertaken at the expense of the Smith family of Hayford Mill. Thereafter however, its fortunes went into sharp decline and in fact it seems to have been closed down for a period because in September 1897, there was held a public meeting of "those agreeable to the opening of the Institute" which was duly revived. Subscriptions had now risen to 6d a month and much effort seems to have gone into making it once again a viable proposition. Magic lantern shows were held; uplifting lectures were given, such as "Palestine – Its People and Its Ways"; Carpet Bowls – costing 16/– were provided; an athletics branch was formed; the McLaren Medal was donated by Mr. J. T. McLaren, Factor of Polamise, for draughts competitions; the local football team, then called Blackwood Rovers used the premises for changing on a Saturday and training during the week, all for 1/–. The committee was helped in its efforts by money from Cambusbarron Horticultural Funds and the Penny Saving Bank, both of which appear to have folded after Hayford

Mills had ceased production.

The most popular pastime in the Institute was, however, its summer ice table – a kind of miniature curling game, played in a long wooden table, with a polished surface, along which small stones, were skimmed into a head as in curling. Such was the passion generated by this game that several members were suspended at various times for unruly conduct during competition.

Also popular were the concerts held several times during the year. One of 22 March 1905, consisted of, amongst others, Mr. McHattie giving *Four Jolly Whistlers*, mandoline selections from Messrs. Aitken and Reid and *The Bonnie Braes O' Airlie* by Mr. C. P. Stevenson. Such concerts often preceded the annual prize giving ceremony.

The winners of 1906 were:
Summer Ice Championship:

1 Mr. Jas. McConnachie, who received a badge donated by Mr. Goodwin

2 Mr. J. Hilton, who received cuff-links to the value of 6/–.

Winners of the monthly summer ice tournaments and their prizes were:

R. Gray, who won a pipe given by Mr. Sanderson; Jas. Greenwood who won a stick (walking?) donated by the Rev. Low; and Mr. J. Greenwood, who won a badge donated by himself. The domino champion was Wm. Allan whose 82 points earned him a knife, to the value of 3/–.

In 1907 however, Cambusbarron United Free Church successfully appealed to Major Murray of Polmaise to have the ground upon which the Institute was built as the site for a new Church. That the Institute did not protest about this suggests that once again it was proving difficult to sustain village interest in the organisation or that the actual building was now wearing badly (it was wooden and had been first erected 80 years previously). Negotiations were begun in the hope of a joint venture, firstly with St. Ninians Kirk Session who were considering building a hall in the village and then with Jas. Drummond of Westerlands, to make use of the old U.F. Church at the foot of the Brae (the former Mill). Both were unsuccessful, St. Ninians wishing to proceed on their own, while the cost of adapting the old, church would have been too high.

Eventually in 1911, on a feu from Major Murray, an iron and wooden building was erected at the foot of the Brae on the site now occupied by the Social Club. Its cost was met by some money received from the sale of remains of the old building, plus donations from villagers, whose names and donations were entered onto a framed painting of a tree with spaces on the leaves for names of donors. Unfortunately this interesting piece of village history was lost or destroyed when the Institute was enlarged into the Social Club.

This new, revised Institute was opened on Saturday 28 October 1911, by Major Murray of Polmaise. It cost £261.18.3$^1/_2$ to buy and erect (only £120 had been raised and the remainder had to be borrowed).

The loan however, was quickly paid off by further donations, principally from Major Murray of Polmaise, Seton Steuart, Robertson, factor, Bearside and Provost Taylor of Clydebank, a Cambusbarron native.

Institute activities then proceeded apace. An interesting innovation to the usual round of draughts, summer ice matches and other activities was the introduction of a shooting range which stretched in tunnel fashion out of the back of the building and into the banking there. There were the usual small controversies that such activities generate; in 1913 for example, A. (Sandy) Gall was stripped of his title of champion shot (and of the silver spoon that was his prize) because "he had allowed his arm to rest of the floor" during competition.

The war, however distant, also touched the affairs of the Institute. Indoor bowls could not be introduced as the manufacturers were unable to obtain wood because of the demand for it caused by the war; village men in France were sent gifts of cigarettes by the Institute Committee; more sombrely, on November 1914, a letter was sent to Major Murray of Polmaise sympathising "with regard to the present uncertain fate of his son". He had in fact been killed. After the war fortnightly "Brains Trust" meetings were initiated by Robert Grierson and James Jackson who debated the question of "Will Britain Follow Other Great European Powers Into Decay?". The topics of other evenings included "The Temperance Question", "The League of Nations", "Newspapers and their Importance".

Despite this impression of energy and enthusiasm things were not going well. There were complaints of rowdy behaviour and gambling. The Institute went into debt. Finally at a public meeting on 7 December 1925, the Committee resigned and handed over care of the premises to the Trustees, after the failure of an appeal "to villagers" to guarantee 3/– each to keep the Institute open. Following this the Institute, as a thriving concern, was finished. The Trustees met annually, only as a formality. Occasional use was made of the building by Girl Guides in 1926 and by an Athletic Club in 1935. On two occasions in 1937 and again in 1942 it was occupied as a temporary home – at a rent of 5/– a week – by two villagers. During the Second World War, it was let to the A.R.P. at £10 p.a., but it was in fact never used by them. Such intermittent letting continued after the War, though by this time the Institute was controlled by a Social Services Committee, elected at a public meeting of 30 March 1942, to consider the future uses of the building. They were responsible for all public property financed by public subscription in the village and general village affairs. The building, perhaps because of its deteriorating condition or size, was not put to any extensive use, though the Committee[2] appear to have been energetic: a Welcome Home programme was planned and financed for the welcome of returning servicemen and women; a permanent football pitch was eventually acquired in 1947 for the village team; the County Education Department was urged to begin evening classes in the village; and small but nevertheless important village concerns such as the condition of the War Memorial, and the Church Clock became the responsibility of the Committee.

In 1964 these responsibilities were taken over by the Committee of Cambusbarron Social Club which opened that year in what had formerly been the Popular Institute. A licence was obtained, the building was renovated and in 1968 (and in the years thereafter) enlarged considerably as a place of entertainment and recreation for villagers.

An undoubted factor in the decline of the Popular Institute was the existence in the village from 1912 of a rival, more commodious attraction: our present Community Centre. Today this building is used for dances, concerts, plays, badminton, library, clinic, public meetings, karate, band practice. It is a valuable asset to the village. Yet its history is a confused and convoluted one which is tied in with the history of our own village church.

When in the 1880s Dr. J. S. Muschet initiated a campaign for a new "Bruce Memorial" Church near to the Chapelwell (see earlier chapter) he not only commissioned plans – for a church with a "crown topped tower like St. Giles in Edinburgh" wrote one who saw them – he also promoted a fund raising campaign and a sum of £467.8.8d was collected. As Dr. Muschet was a member of the Free Church of Scotland, and as that church was the only one with premises in the village, and since these premises – a disused mill, converted in the 1860's to a church – were less than satisfactory, it seems reasonable to suggest that he intended to build a Free Church with the money. Yet it is curious that when the project eventually came to nothing, after Muschet's death in 1886, the money was handed over for safekeeping to St. Ninians Kirk Session – a Church of Scotland body. A reason suggested by the Rev. Adam, United Free Minister in Cambusbarron from 1906, was that St. Ninians "was the only Church Session of secure position in the Parish". The Session of Cambusbarron Free Church at this time was not "of secure position" and indeed the Church was to lose its status and become again, as it had been previously, A Mission Station.

When, however, in 1908, it was decided to build a new United Free Church in the village, St. Ninians Kirk Session refused to surrender the funds that had been collected over twenty years earlier. It was, St. Ninians insisted, a Church of Scotland fund. It seems they were partly correct. Some people contributing to the collection did so in the belief that a Church of Scotland building was to be erected, because of an earlier fund for that purpose, had been started by St. Ninians in the 1870's and over £250 had been collected. The £467.8.8d raised in Cambusbarron in the 1880's was added to this earlier sum.

With some ill feeling towards their neighbours, Cambusbarron United Free Church carried on with their plans and thanks to an outstanding fund raising campaign – including a very successful 3 day Bazaar in the Albert Hall

in October 1908, and a donation of £500 from Mr. Robert Johnstone of Craigview (he also gave the pulpit) [3] – the new church was opened on 11 June 1910 [4] by the Rev. John Young D.D., Moderator of Assembly.

A list of church officers may prove interesting: The Session comprised the Rev. James. A. Adam M.A. as Moderator with Duncan Wilkie, Alex Davidson, Alex Duff (Jnr), Jas. F. Melles, William Robertson, Duncan Robertson, and Wm. Somerville as Session Clerk. The Deacons were: Jas. Taylor, Alex McConnachie, Charles Starkey, John McClumpha (Also Church Officer), John Young, Robert Hanna, William Gilchrist, James Scott, Thomas Tollerton, Robert Erskine and John Gardner. The organist and choir leader was Miss Petrie. There were two services on Sunday, plus a Sunday School or "Sabbath School" as it was called, at 4 pm. and a Bible Class at 5.15.

Cambusbarron Church, the Bruce Memorial, has flourished since 1910. On 16 June 1935, its Silver Jubilee was celebrated when all three ministers who had served there in its first twenty five years – the Reverends Adam, Monteith Davidson and McKinlay – were present. 1960 saw the Golden Jubilee year.

Before the Bruce Memorial was built in 1910, the only place of worship in Cambusbarron was the partly disused mill mentioned perviously. This was acquired in 1860 by the United Free Church of Scotland and converted into what was called a "Mission Station" – not a full church. Its first preacher – again not a full minister – was Mr. Thomas Bruce, a probationer and its first elders Mr. Peter Drummond (the Nursery family) and Mr. Archibald Henderson (who was to serve for the next forty years) and its first communicants were Dr. Muschet, John Kennedy, John Jamieson, Mrs. Kennedy, James Sorley, Mrs. Scott, Joan Smith, David Hunter, Miss Wark, Miss Jane Donaldson, Miss Margaret Donaldson, Miss Paterson, Robert Cowan, Mrs. Cowan, Mrs. Weir, Mrs Sorley, Mrs. Hunter and James Wark.

A report, compiled by a committee of the congregation during its first year, gives us some background to the establishment of the station:

"Before any public ordinances were set up there, it (i.e. Cambusbarron) was the resort, especially on the Sabbath, of the idle and dissolute of the neighbouring towns and villages, and became on these occasions a den of wickedness. . . there is no place of worship in the village but the hall of the Free Church Station. . . the number of persons attending church [5] in these places (this refers to Stirling and St. Ninians) from Cambusbarron is a very small proportion of the population while the number of church-goers is a very large one. It is further ascertained that the population will receive a large accession very soon as mines are to be opened in the neighbourhood. . . For some years a meeting has been maintained in a school-house, capable of holding 80. The average attendance had been 60. Now a handsome and comfortable Hall fitted up and rented can hold 130".

The worshippers included weavers who had worked in the building when it was a mill and who installed their pews where their looms had once been. The pews, along with pulpit and other furnishings were supplied by Dr. Muschet who also owned the building (which was originally erected by the two Cambusbarron men who built Hayford Mill; see earlier chapter – "Work"). Dr. Muschet appears to have been a valuable benefactor to the Station, if at the same time a somewhat difficult one: on one occasion he threatens to withdraw his financial support

for the Station, because of the "non-fulfilment of their pecuniary engagements by certain Free Church men who shall be nameless"; another time he accuses the missionary of neglect and insists that he reside in the village and not in Stirling. To be fair to Muschet, his grumbling perhaps disguises his fervent concern that the Station should flourish and become a proper Church with a Minister of its own. (In the first fifteen years of its existence, the Station had ten "missionaries" all of whom were probationers).

Finally however, Muschet got his wish and the Mission Station became a Church in November 1878. Its first minister was the Rev. Thomas Stewart whose tenure was a tragically short one as he died within the year. Sadly, also, after a bright beginning, the "new" Church did not mature and Cambusbarron reverted to a Mission Station in 1896. With the arrival ten years later of the Rev. Adam, who was an energetic figure, a Church was again established and under Mr. Adam's guidance, the new Bruce Memorial was built.

As the 1861 report above states, before 1860 there was no place of worship in Cambusbarron. The village was part of St. Ninians Parish and the church in the village of that name, a mile

The Brae. Only the house on the extreme left still stands.

The Brae Cambusbarron.

Murray Place (looking towards Main Street). The houses on the right have been demolished. Those on the left still stand.

and a half from Cambusbarron Cross, *was* Cambusbarron's church[6]. Not until the 19th century was well advanced and its population grew, could the village sustain its own church. Before then it was less a village and more a hamlet, or "toun" – a small collection of cottages, originally gathered around or adjacent to arable or pastoral land. (Visitors to Scotland even as late as 18th century remarked on the absence of villages, which were so common in England). An early map (1817) shows most of Cambusbarron's houses on the Brae and along the present Main Street, with a few more on the present Murray Place. The North End is largely empty, suggesting, perhaps that the village grew as a "farm toun" with the flatter land of Hayford, the North End, Birkhill and Coneypark used for farming and the rising slopes of the Gillies Hill for dwellings.

The inhabitants of this earlier Cambusbarron especially in the 17th century, found their lives to a remarkable degree, at least to our modern eyes, scrutinised by the Kirk Session of St. Ninians. After the Reformation, the new church sought to establish on earth a "Godly Commonwealth" where, under the guidance of the Church, men would lead lives which should come as near as possible to a reflection of God's Kingdom in Heaven. The building of such a visionary society allowed the church wide-ranging powers against those who fell by the wayside. In 1654, for example, two Cambusbarron women, Janet Chiney and Janet Neilson appeared before the Session, accused of giving birth to illegitimate children "begotten by English soldiers". (This seems to have been a common transgression during the Cromwellian occupation. For some time General Monck, one of the Protector's Chief Officers, encamped his army near Cambusbarron).

Nor was the Kirk partial in its justice. The gentry were not spared their blushes; in 1659 James Seton of Touch was ordered to make public repentance for his fornication with Barbara Fleming [7].

More serious (and less seldom committed – or discovered?) sins were adultery and blasphemy; sabbath-breaking was slightly more common and on one occasion at least, the Session investigated a case involving alleged witchcraft in 1703, when Agnes Law of Cambusbarron complained that John Douglas and his wife had called her a witch. Douglas had apparently said to his wife, "Blood her and she will do you no evil", which his complaisant wife did. In many of these cases one is taken aback at the eagerness of "friends" and neighbours of the accused to come forward and testify against him/her.

The Kirk Session continued to monitor the morals of its parishioners until less than eighty years ago – till 1902, in fact.

But the Kirk had a less stern face and one class of society had particular reason to be grateful to it: the poor. The principle that every parish should be responsible for its poor was a product of a 16th century law. The Reformers of the Church had hoped to use tithes or rents of the old church properties to sustain the poor, but that patrimony was diverted by the nobility into their own pockets and the method of providing relief for the poor in the 17th, 18th and 19th centuries was left to the discretion of individual parishes. In St. Ninians Parish poor relief was provided principally from the following:

1 Church door collections; [8]

2 Voluntary contributions from heritors (the chief landowners of the parish). This happened for example, in 1800 when the heritors agreed to a 10/– levy on themselves, plus voluntary contributions from their tenants, to afford relief to those many unable to buy bread because of the high price of grain;

3 Mortifications or bequests to the poor by wealthy members of the Parish. Besides William Wordie's Parish bequest (see chapter 5) the poor of our Parish benefited from the Greenock Mortification. James Greenock lived on the farm of Whitehouse, Cambusbarron and was a devoted Christian and lay preacher. When he died in 1813 he left property plus a sum of money, the income from which was to help the poor. Specifically he hoped the money would be used "for purchasing Bibles to poor scholars or such other pious uses as to the said Minister and Kirk Session shall seem most useful and expedient"…and…" the sum of £10 to a schoolmaster to be settled at the village of Cambusbarron". Interest on a sum of £400, collected by the Parish Minister in London in 1747 when he was attempting to get compensation for his recently blown up Church, also went to the needy.

4 The fines sometimes imposed on sinners. In October 1746, Isabell Bennet was fined 16/– for fornication. The following year Thomas Thomson had to pay £5; (was he a hardened sinner perhaps, or were fines levied according to financial circumstances?)

5 From the hire of mortcloths. These were palls or cloths which covered the coffin during a funeral service. It was important to the families of the deceased that the funeral rites be carried out in a seemly manner and the mortcloth was a vital element in those rites. In our Parish the bereaved family had a choice of mortcloths. In November 1776, for example, Mrs. Janet Wilsone of Murrayshall – a genteel household – paid 5/– for the best mortcloth. In February 1785, the clerk recorded the receipt of 4/– for the 2nd mortcloth from the piper's wife at Touch. The cheapest and presumably the smallest, for it was used so often for children, cost 1/6d. This was the sum paid in July 1775 by Alexander Aikman, Cambusbarron for the 1st and 2nd mortcloths for his two children; and what of the feelings of John Cowie of Clayhills in Cambusbarron on 15th February 1776 when he paid 4/6d for *three* of the smallest cloths for his dead children? Life was a tenuous and fragile thing in those times. What dreadful catastrophe – accident or illness – required *twelve* cloths, eight for children, four for adults, on December 2nd 1779? However, the revenue from these hires helped to keep many of the other poor from the grave.

6 Legal assessments – heritors had the authority to impose a legal assessment on property, but as this could become complicated and arouse argument, it was not often attempted in this parish. One such occasion is nevertheless recorded in 1787. The assessment was rated at 16/– for every £100, half was to be paid by the tenant, half by the landowner. Collectors were appointed to get the money in. In Cambusbarron, one was William Graham of Carsebonnie (Kersebonny Farm?) The scheme must have been successful, as it continued for some years and future Cambusbarron collectors were George Donaldson, John Watson and Alexander Buchanan in 1800. In the same year the heritors appointed James Greenock, one of their members, and William Crawford to investigate those poor in Cambusbarron who wanted a meal at a reduced rate to work out "how much each could pay according to his means".

Cheap food in times of scarcity was one way in which the Cambusbarron poor were offered relief. Others received a fixed "pension", paid perhaps once a month – "Andrew Wordie's blind lass in Cambusbarron" for example, probably an orphan, was receiving 12/– a month in 1746 – while others again received sums on an ad hoc basis. Either way, the Poor Roll makes for poignant reading:

"8 June 1746, to the Craigforth foundling, 16/–".
"10 July 1746, to two gentlemen in need, £3".
"17 September 1746, to Gentle Jane [9], 3/–".
"2 July 1747, to John McAllister, to buy a Bible, £1. 2/–".
"2 July 1747, to William McLean for a coffin for a child (again this is a sadly recurring entry) 15/–".
"8 October 1747, to a wounded Dragoon 2/–".
"6 November 1747, to John Junckin, to help him to college £18.18/–".
"7 March 1748, to John Malcom's son, to buy him a coat and shirt 12/–".
"13 March 1748, to a master of a ship taken by the Spanish, 15/–".
Sometimes the recipients are unnamed:
"16 April 1758, to one object at Cambusbarron 12/–", or in July 1759, "14 objects" in Cambusbarron receive £8.18/– divided amongst themselves; shortly afterwards, a second divided of £13.16/– went to "23 objects".

Before the report of the 1843 Commission on Poor Relief and the ensuing Act of Parliament which removed from the Kirk the task of assisting the poor (a statutory assessment system was introduced and Parochial Boards created) the only means of relief for the needy had for almost 300 years been supplied by the Kirk [10]. It's easy, when we think of the harsh, discipline of that body in the centuries after the Reformation to forget its more compassionate face.

In 1910, the resentment against St. Ninians Kirk Session felt by some United Free members in Cambusbarron must have been exacerbated when St. Ninians announced the intention of erecting a Church of Scotland in Cambusbarron – using the money collected during Dr. Muschet's time. The question that inevitably presents itself to us today is this: was the attitude of the Kirk Session a reasonable response to a need[11] in Cambusbarron for a Church of Scotland? Or was St. Ninians indulging in some petty ecclesiastical rivalry with the Free Church in the village? It is difficult to avoid this second view. If a Church of Scotland were needed in Cambusbarron, why was it so especially needed in 1910, just as a new Free Kirk was being built? The same question can be asked about an earlier occasion in the 1870's when St. Ninians Session[12] considered building a church in the village – just after the Free Church Mission had established itself and thereafter did little to pursue this until 1910. In the event a Parish Hall and not a church was built and a degree of good sense (much of it supplied by Robert Grierson, a St. Ninians member) arrived at, as some foresaw a day when the Free Church might wish to rejoin the larger organisation – as happened in 1929 – and two churches of the same denomination, barely 100 yards apart would have been would have been a telling comment on parochial petty-mindedness. Yet even after 1929, when the Bruce Memorial was Church of Scotland, a degree of acrimony continued over the ownership of the Parish Hall, as it was called. In 1939 the Rev. McKinley asked to what use the Hall had been put to by St.

Ninians and declared that is was used very rarely for religious services and more often for what he termed "frivolous entertainments". He went on to cite wedding receptions where alcohol was served as examples. Throughout the 1940's, however, local Presbytery opinion began to favour a transfer of the Hall to Cambusbarron Church – a Presbytery minute of 12 December so recommended.

By 1945, St. Ninians felt able to offer Cambusbarron the chance to buy the building. In the event it was obtained by the local authority Stirling County Council, under whose auspices the Hall was administered by Cambusbarron Social Services Committee. It now comes under the jurisdiction of Cambusbarron Community Association.

This chapter has already described how the Popular Institute began by offering villagers some intellectual diversion from the hardships of day to day life. Other more frivolous entertainments flourished. "Hurley hawkey" – sliding down a hillside using the polished skull of a cow like a sledge – was an ancient children's pleasure, carried out on the southern slope of the Gillies Hill between "the Slack" and "the Bonnety Tree". Curling is another sport engaged in by our village forefathers. In the recent past Bearside Pond on Polmaise Estate was the home of Bearside Curling Club. An old ruined curling house can still be seen there. In the early years of this century unemployed men were paid to do odd jobs at the curling ponds, such as clearing away snow from the rinks, or boiling – for the players – potatoes sent down from the Castle, or making ready the artificial curling rink nearby – the tarred area, often mistaken for tennis courts. A layer of water was sprayed onto this surface, allowed to freeze and then another layer was spread on, and so on. A primitive form of floodlighting carried by iron poles around this area was powered by gas, relayed from Polmaise Castle. (Gas had been supplied to the village in 1846).

Curlers on Bearside Ponds, Polmaise.(The clubhouse is under trees on the right-hand side)

Another illuminative innovation badly frightened one of the workers when one dark evening before a bonspiel he saw a glow proceeding down the Castle avenue, accompanied by an eerie hooting sound. This was, in fact one of the curlers from the Castle carrying an early electric torch, one whose power had to be generated by an attached footpump which caused the weird noise.

Curling was played in Cambusbarron, however, long before the time of electricity or gas. Ancient curling stones have been found in Coneypark Nursery, on the site of what was once called "Davie's Bog"; others have been unearthed from sites at Birkhill and the Kings Park where lochans, now dried up, have existed at one time.

Cambusbarron Brass Band engaged much popularity both in the village and elsewhere at the turn of the century. Among their players were Colin Lennox, George Marshall, Andrew Lennox, Robert Dalgleish, James Bryce and James Ferguson. Besides competitions they performed at many social events in the village calendar: each New Year's Day they played in the crossroads formed by the Main Street, Murray Place and the Brae (now blocked off to traffic); on Coronation Day 1902 they marched through the village with Robert Grierson and the entire school to the Popular Institute where Mr. Murray of Polmaise planted a special Coronation Tree (a Norwegian Maple). The silver mounted spade was presented to Mrs. Murray and the company then marched, band at the front, to Polmaise Home Farm where a pleasant afternoon was spent.

Such outings were popular and most popular of all was the Berry Trip. This was really the Sunday School outing, when the village children marched from Cambusbarron with the Band, or in later years with a piper leading the way, down Snowdon Place to Westerlands, the home of the Drummond family who had begun the Sunday School. Here they were presented with bags of goose-berries and large rhubarb tarts. After games and races, the trippers marched homeward, carrying bags of cakes and sweets. Innocent, homely pleasures again, but hugely enjoyed.

Like the Drummonds, the Murrays of Polmaise occasionally offered philanthropic hospitality towards the less well off of

Cambusbarron. In June 1905 for example, a garden party was held at the Castle for tenants, workers and friends. The occasion was the Laird's birthday. After an illuminated address on behalf of all the tenants was presented by the oldest, Robert Walls of Kersemill, the guests were allowed free run of the grounds, some picnicking by the ornamental lake, others visiting the model dairy at the Home Farm. And in January 1903, the servants, estate workers and sundry other locals were entertained to a supper dance at the Castle, the Company being led off in dancing by the Colonel and Mr. Galloway, the housekeeper, and Mrs. Murray and Mr. Tanner, the butler.

Other ambrosial evenings were certainly enjoyed by Cambusbarron men in the less magnificent surroundings of the village public house. In late Victorian and Edwardian times, there were two pubs in the village, in the most direct competition each other, as they occupied adjoining buildings. One, called "The Forester's Arms" was in the premises which are still occupied today as a public house. Happily, it has retained its original name. The licensee was a Mrs. Goodall. Next door was the second pub, owned by Jas. Melles, the village blacksmith and called " The Star Inn". If the white paintwork above the ground floor is studied carefully, the name of the last proprietor (he arrived in 1906) – "Frederick Anderson – Licensed to sell Wines, Spirits and Beers" – is just decipherable.

These pubs offered an alternative, if, in the eyes of some, a somewhat less decorous distraction from the cares of everyday life. Saturday evenings – paynight at the Mill – led to some wild behaviour. As early as 1861, a petition from some Cambusbarron residents was presented to the Commissioners of Supply in Stirling (an early County Council) requesting the appointment of a police constable to the village. This was not granted until 1881, when the Committee reported that "the village has a population of 1230, principally of the working classes and there is in addition a large number of operatives in the Mills". One constable from Stirling who was occasionally stationed in the village on Saturday evenings, was no longer adequate and the appointment of a full time policeman, at a wage of 22/6d per week was made the following year, 1882[13]. His work was particularly busy during the building of the North

Cambusbarron Boy Scouts, dressed in the Murray tartan, photographed in St. Ninians Road. (The house in the background still stands)

Third Reservoir (1906–1909) when the two village pubs were much frequented by the many Irish navvies who worked on the Reservoir. (One was found dead in Murrays' wood after a night's drinking. Trying to make his way back to North Third he had apparently slipped, knocking himself unconscious and froze to death. This incidentally is the origin of the cairn in the woods just before the fields).

Pleasant times were also enjoyed in the pubs. "The Star Inn" was occasionally the scene of small scale social functions, such as that in June 1903 when James Jack, who was emigrating to Canada, was seen on his way by his friends with several refreshments and the presentation of a Gladstone Bag. Balaklava Day was also celebrated there and on that day in October 1892, the 39th anniversary, two village veterans of the battle, Corporal Charles Inglis and Private John Watson, both of the 93rd Sutherland Highlanders, were toasted there by their friends, after ex-Private Watson had given an account of the fighting and the part played in it by "The Thin Red Line". (Another Cambusbarron man, James Robertson,

had fought at Inkerman as a member of the Rifle Brigade). Drinkers derived added benefits from the close proximity of the two pubs: when the whisky salesman arrived, it was the tradition of the time that he stood a round of nips for everyone who happened to be in the bar. Needless to say, he became a well-known and popular figure in the village and "The Star Inn" was usually thick with custom for his arrival. Having toasted his health the clientele would then take their leave, only to immediately install themselves next door, where the poor traveller was obliged to perform once more.

More abstemious pleasures were enjoyed in the Band Hall, the ruin of which can still be made out in the space of ground between Alma and Glenmoray Houses.[14] Here met for many years the Band of Hope ("Band of Devils", according to the Rev. Adam who found their obstreperous behaviour of the young people less than seemly). Here also Saturday night dances were held, as they were – surprising when the limited space is considered – in the ante room at the Marne Cafe, owned in later times by Mr. Giannandrea. (The same area was often used as a billiard room).

After 1911 the Parish Hall became the venue for many such social functions. In February 1929, for example, there was held there the tenth annual reunion Dinner and Dance of the Cambusbarron and District ex-Servicemen Association. Music was supplied by Drummond's Orchestra from Bannockburn and the event was presided over by the Association's Chairman, Mr. David Taylor. (The Association had been established after the War and were well represented in the War Memorial Committee. The Memorial was unveiled on October 3rd 1920, by Major Murray of Polmaise).

Village branches of the Boys Brigade and the Scouts also flourished in Cambusbarron, the former meeting in the B.B. Hut which stood where the present Church Hut is sited, the latter being kitted out by Major Murray in kilts of Murray tartan.

"The Cambron Players", a group of amateur thespians brought much enjoyment to themselves, pleasure to others and distinction to Cambusbarron in the early Fifties with their successes in the Scottish Community Drama Association Competition. The Y.M.C.A., a Horticultural Society (one of the oldest village groups, it folded immediately after the Mill closure, but was revived in 1903); The Burns Club, a Mutual Improvement Society, an Athletic Club, a Cycling Club, which was formed in the bar of the Woodside Hotel, Doune after a few village men had cycled there in pursuit of refreshment in October 1894, a Scooter Club, have all existed at various times.

Two sports, however, which have endured better than most have been football and bowling. Cambusbarron Bowling Club was opened on 5th July 1903 by Mrs James Drummond of Westerlands who was presented with the silver jack she had thrown. It was a memorable village occasion, with a large crowd present and the Brass Band playing. The ground, formerly called Woodside Park, had been granted at a nominal rent by Colonel Murray (who was unable to be present because of illness; he died the following month). The turf had been laid at a cost of £300. The Club's first President was J. T. McLaren, factor at Polmaise, John Miller was the Secretary, P. Robertson was the Treasurer, R. Grierson the Vice-President. Its first champion was James

Penny. The skips were J. Goodwin, R. Liddel, J. Lennox and Edward Watson and annual subscription was 7/6d.

The first Clubhouse was erected in 1907 (previously a shelter had been used) the year after the Club received its flagpole – a long awaited gift from Murray of Polmaise, who had promised it when the Club won its first match.[15] This first Clubhouse, opened by Jas. Murray of Polmaise, was enlarged in 1962 and more recently in 1978, the Club opened its new extension, much of the work being undertaken by the members in their own time

That the name of Cambusbarron has, in the past 25 years or so, came to be widely recognised throughout Scotland, owes much to the achievements of its village football club, Cambusbarron Rovers. Three times, in 1968, 1969 and 1978, they have won the Scottish Amateur Cup, once in 1974 they were runners-up and twice more in, 1972 and 1977, they were semi-finalists. An outstanding record; that over 600 clubs now enter the national tournament. Moreover, the Club has won many league championships, the East of Scotland Cup and a host of local trophies.[16]

The Rovers began in 1960 but they have a long history of footballing antecedents in the village – Cambusbarron F.C., Polmaise Rovers, and the earliest, Blackwood Rovers are all ancestors of our modern club. And not only has the name changed over the years, but so has their home. Mill Road Park was acquired in 1947; previously the game was played (a) in the present public park (b) Woodside Park where the Bowling Green is now (c) in a field called Hayfield Park presently occupied by the Yetts and Cauldhame Crescent. Hayfield Park was in fact the Club's first home and they opened it on Saturday 23rd October 1892, with a game against the village Brass Band. Surprisingly, despite having marched to the Park and played there for some time before the game began, the Band won. This inauspicious start was merely an omen for what was to come, as the Blackwood lost their first six matches against "foreign" opposition, usually by high margins, such as a 1–8 home reserve by Stirling Emmet in the Stirling and District Junior F.A. Cup. But gradually the team improved and gained a reputation no less deserved than that of their modern counterparts:

In the winter of 1894, for example, they were un–defeated in ten games, beating such renowned opposition as Bannockburn Battlefield, Alloa Hearts, Tullibody and Kings Park reserves and Doune F.C.. Their run ended in a controversial sequence of cup ties versus Stirling Athletic. Let the football correspondent of the *Stirling Journal* explain:

> "If there is one thing more than another calculated to turn Junior Association Football into ridicule it is the inevitable protest which crops up in connection with so many cup-ties. . . It will be remembered that on Saturday week, the Blackwood Rovers beat Stirling Athletic in the 2nd round of the Junior Cup by 3 goals to 2 after a game in which the City of Rock men did nothing to impress the onlookers with any great claim to gentlemanly conduct or superior football players. But with sublime effrontery they had protests in the air before they left the ground and canvassed the town and district for the necessary votes to get the tie played over again, which they managed by 6 votes to 2. I hear the Rovers are so thoroughly disgusted that they intend scratching; but we wouldn't advise them doing any such thing. The only well grounded protest which could be urged in the matter was one by the Rovers against having to play such opposition, or by the spectators for being asked to pay to look at them."

But pay spectators did, to the tune of more than £5 in "gate money". Since admission was 3d this meant that over 400 spectators must have watched the next match – which Stirling won 3–1. (Ladies, incidentally were admitted free).

In the 1900s the Club changed its name to the now famous Cambusbarron Rovers. Their reputation as a good team grew: on New Year's Day 1904, for example, they beat a combined Army/Navy team 5–1 and by 1910, the Journal's correspondent was recommending – "The Rovers to go further afield and fix up matches with teams of outstanding merit". In December of the same year, after a run which included a 13–2 win over Dunblane, 10 – 0 versus Bannockburn and 9 – 2 versus Forest Rovers, the Journal declared: that "the Scottish Cup is sure to find a place on Kelly's sideboard". Unfortunately, like others before and after him, club captain Kelly found

the fantasy of football success fade when confronted with harsh reality, and the cup had to wait another 58 years before coming to Cambusbarron. The composition of the club at this time is known. The President was John K. Thomson, vice-president M. Neil, secretary A. Stenhouse, the treasurer D. Holmes and the executive Messrs. Dale, Cuthbert, Wyatt and Robertson. A typical team was: Ferguson, Watson, McMillan, Kelly, McIntosh, Donaldson, Allan, Greenwood, Robertson, Donald, Dale.

Shop life in Cambusbarron has not changed as drastically as other features of its recent past. Yet changes there have been. Mrs M. Rycroft, a granddaughter of Duncan Wilkie who opened a grocer's shop in Cambusbarron (he borrowed £100 which he repaid within the year) in 1876 recalls family memories of her grandfather's business:

"In the shop my grandfather kept red-herring, salt herring and ling. He blended his own whisky, (the smell enhancing the general atmosphere of the Main Street). He skimmed his own cheeses and boned his hams; he kept paraffin, syrup and treacle in wooden casks in the outhouse and black soap and loom salt too. In the garden was an old shed that originally had been the slaughterhouse. It had an earthen floor and lots of beams with cleeks and hooks on them."

Several village tradesmen, no matter their particular business, kept pigs: even Willie Jack, the village slater and chimney sweep, who lived in the Main Street and John Melles, the blacksmith of Sunnybank did so. A hundred years ago Wilkie's shop was at 18 Main Street. In the North End were Tam Stewart's, the fishman and Davidson, the fruiterer. Elsewhere were: Alexander Allison, shoemaker; Cambusbarron Co-operative; John Cullens, butcher; Donaldson Brothers, joiners; T. Easton, shoemaker; Mrs James McGregor, licensed grocer; Matthew Shanks, the Brae, was village newsagent, stationer, draper and postmaster (he received 6d for every telegram delivered to Touch House). J. Walls was a dressmaker; George Watson, shoemaker; Robert Taylor was a tailor and clothier and James Taylor a grocer. Both these brothers also built their own shops, one in the West End, now converted to a house, the other continuing as a shop in Birthill Road.

57

The West End in the 1950s.

An earlier (1860s) list of village businesses offered the following: a Co-op, managed by James Taylor,[16] Wm. Cowie, bootmaker; John Donaldson, joiner; John Gilchrist, dairyman; J. Lammond, coalman and flesher; Eliza Johnstone, grocer; William McCallum, baker and grocer; John McGregor, grocer, contractor and publican – he was one of the earlier owners of the "Star Inn"; Duncan McIntosh, also a publican – (next door?); Alexander McLauchlan, tea dealer; Duncan McNaughton, grocer; Mrs Thomas Reilly, grocer; Henry Jaffray, post office; Peter Stewart, tailor; Alex Walls, coalman and Mrs White "provisions dealer".

At other times during the last quarter of the 19th century, other small businessmen, besides these above catered for Cambusbarron's needs. David Craigan was another licensee of "The Star Inn" sometime after John McGregor; Robert Miller supplied milk to the district from his North End premises, but must have done so in competition with Daniel Robertson, designated as of "Hayford"; Duncan McKenzie was a

butcher, Laurence Steedman, a grocer, Jane Wells, a draper. Even the last need of all was catered for by the village hearse, which was kept in a building between the Church and the schoolhouse, part of which can still be seen today, called the Coach-house.

Cambusbarron life at the turn of the century had nevertheless a less edifying side to it. There were, of course, as there are always, the petty nuisances of village life. In October 1892, for example, Glenmoray Burn once again burst its banks at the bottom of the Brae, causing much distress and considerable damage to property. The gas street lights were the subject of repeated complaint, the most common of which that they were often unable to be lit. An explanation may lie in the fact that "their upkeep is got by public subscription".

More seriously ill-health and industrial accidents were more prevalent then. We have already seen how school attendance could be badly affected by such diseases as scarlet fever or diptheria which are thankfully no longer the menace they once were. And at least six men were killed and several seriously injured in separate accidents during the construction of the North Third and Earlsburn Reservoirs (1906–09). The miners in the community suffered injury and occasional loss of life in pit accidents. Domestic crime featured prominently in the local press. Breach of the peace, drunkenness and wife assault were usually penalised by a 10/– fine or seven days (though one case of cruelty to a horse led to a 20/– fine or ten days. Was it a valuable horse?). And as always, there were the poor.

Even as late as 1913, a man was arrested in Cambusbarron for begging (he got 5/– or 3 days). In the following year the names of 14 people from the village appeared on the Parish Poor Roll. By the end of the War there were still 6 names. For the most destitute, there was sanctuary in the Poor House (in Stirling) but also the sense of shame that accompanied one's entry to it. The less desperately poor received a fixed sum weekly according to their needs. In 1906, for instance, 5 villagers were receiving 2/6 a week: 2 others were given 5/– and others again received varying sums.

These benefits were paid from assessments made of property by the Parochial Board set up after the 1840 Act had removed from the Church the responsibility for Poor Relief. These assessments, one half to be paid by the owner, one half by the tenant, were not always met, especially by the latter. The Church, incidentally, continued an interest in the poor. In 1853 five Cambusbarron children were to be sent to the village school at the expense of the Kirk, as their families were too poor to pay the fees. The same year it was agreed that the graves of "paupers belonging to the Parish shall be dug for 1/–; the first coffin in each grave to be placed 10 feet deep".

Of more practical benefit was the £26.1.7d Cambusbarron Relief Fund distributed in April 1897 to distressed villagers still suffering from the effects of the Mills closure six months before.

Yet the most enduring picture of Cambusbarron life in the years up to 1914 is one of an active outgoing community – a community which in many ways clearly led a life different from ours today, but one which despite its many hardships saw ordinary people more and more take an intelligent and enthusiastic interest in the social and political forces that influenced their lives.

In February 1908, for example, a lively public meeting in the School discussed one of the important issues of the day, tariff reform, when a Mrs Fletcher, the main speaker, referred to the empty Cambusbarron Mills as a result of unfair foreign competition. She was vigorously opposed by James Jackson, who saw the fate of the Mill as a result of bad business practice by the Company. At the end of the same year, an election meeting witnessed a verbal confrontation between John Brady, an unemployed farm labourer and Major Murray of Polmaise who, claimed Brady, kept 100 acres of his estate uncultivated while so many who went without work could be gainfully employed. In Mrs Grierson, the village had an early advocate of feminism who organised meetings of the W.S.P.U.[17] in the schoolhouse.

This pre-war world, soon to be savagely shattered, had about it also an innocence and simplicity of outlook which readily lend themselves to scorn and mockery in our more "sophisticated" and "advanced" times. *The Stirling Journal's* words of 13th August 1914, when it commended Cambusbarron Boy Scouts for "performing the very necessary duty of guarding Touch Waterworks" raise images of kilted village boys scanning the Touch skyline for Zeppelins or German saboteurs. It seems the very stuff of *Ripping Yarns.*

Yet our amusement should be tinged with envy, and, perhaps anxiety. For that innocence and simplicity are attractive qualities to a modern world which, despite its material progress, has lost much that is precious since the time of our forefathers. The world of the past was to most of its people a hard, hard world; but, in Cambusbarron as elsewhere, made bearable and indeed enjoyable by people coming together and working for the common good. If we, in our pursuit of material comfort, have exchanged idealism for cynicism, enthusiasm for apathy, and above all, if we have elevated self above community – if there is, as we have been told, "no such thing as society" then we have failed to learn the principal lesson of the past. Our modern Cambusbarron, for all its blemishes, remains a most pleasant place. We who live here owe a debt of thanks to the many, named and anonymous, whose labours down the years, have made it so. And we have a responsibility to continue their work.

1 Or alternatively it may have been Cambusbarron Subscription School's last teacher Alex. McCallum.

2 This first S.S.C. comprised R. Neilson, C. Bryson, D. Hughes, T. Stewart, A. Sneddon, W. Johns, J. Taylor and D. Low. In addition the Minister (Mr Webster), the County Councillor , (Col. E.P. Buchanan of Touch – though at this time P.O.W.), and the District Councillor (John Donaldson) were also statutory members.

3 The internal clock was giver by Duncan Wilkie, a grocer in the village and the front was presented by Ladies Juveniles Work Party. A bible was presented to the minister by James Jackson. The architects were McLuckie and Walker of Stirling, and the building, made of Polmaise stone, cost £1,000 plus £200 to buy the old Popular Institute. The clock bell was inaugurated by James Mann who cut a silk ribbon with a pair of silver scissors – presented by Hepting and Farrer, the clockmakers – to set the machinery going. Gardener and Stirling were the masons.

4 The Foundation stone had been laid in August 1909, by Major Murray of Polmaise. Sealed in the stone were: a copy of that day's *Scotsman* and that week's copies of the Stirling papers, the *Journal*, *Sentinel* and *Observer*; a list of the members of the Congregation: the annual report for 1909; the Bazaar programme; silver and copper coins; a church magazine; a programme for the day's ceremony and an invitation ticket; and a list of subscribers. Prominent at the ceremony also were two ancient banners villagers had carried in earlier times advocating

   (1) the repeal of the Corn Laws and

   (2) the Reform Bill.

5 It should be emphasised that the Parish Church for Cambusbarron residents for hundreds of years – until 1929 – continued to be that of St. Ninians. This was of course

a Church of Scotland. The above mentioned Station belonged to the Free Church of Scotland, who had broken away from the established church in 1843.

6 A list of male heads of families who were members at St. Ninians in 1835 numbered 33, viz:

Alexander Donaldson	weaver
William Sutherland	labourer
Robert Jamieson	weaver
Robert Ferguson	labourer
David Robertson	weaver
Robert Robertson	labourer
Francis Thomson	weaver
William Jenkins	miner
James Jamieson	weaver
James Reid	shoemaker
Peter Bryce	weaver
William Henderson	gardener
James Buchan	weaver
James Aitchison	spinner
John Jamieson Sen.	weaver
James Donaldson	baker
John Jamieson Jnr.	weaver
Daniel McDermaid	teacher
Alan Ure	weaver
George Learmonth	dancing master
Andrew Stewart	weaver
William Drummond (Coney Park)	seedsman
William Bryce	weaver
William Maxwell	labourer
George MacKay	farm servant
John Andrew	farmer
James Anderson (Hollanbush)	farmer
John Mitchell	labourer
John Murdoch (Clayhills)	farmer
John McNab	labourer
John McNie	labourer
Patrick Muschet of Birkhill	

7 The customary punishment was to sit on the stool of repentance before the entire congregation. Sometimes it was financial. Agnes Miller, a servant of John Wordie of Cambusbarron was summoned before the session in 1743 to explain why, her banns having been called, she had not yet married. She was fined 10/–. Later, when the marriage had in fact taken place, her husband, Robert Jaffray, a weaver of Hayford in Cambusbarron, asked for the fine to be

returned. He received (note: not poor Agnes who'd paid it) a crown (half the sum, i.e. 5/− or 25p), the session retaining the other crown as the marriage had not been celebrated within a year of the banns being called.

While many "sinners" were married couples, guilty of what the Kirk called "antenuptial fornication", a proportion were unmarried mothers whose illegitimate children were easily recognisable proof of their "guilt". The fathers quite often escaped undetected, unfairly leaving the poor mother to bear the sting of public disapproval. Sometimes when the father was named so that the escapee's new parish would be informed and he would be summoned before its Session to explain himself.

8 Those members from Cambusbarron who were generous contributors in 1683, for example, included: William Wordie; John Aikman; John Douglas; John Stevenson; John Gilliespie and James Whyte, all weavers; John Cowan "Gilliehill"; John Thomson, "proportioner".

9 "Gentle" was often a euphemism for "insane".

10 As it had been, of course, by the Old Church before the Reformation.

11 Before 1912 Church of Scotland services were held monthly in the Primary School.

12 And to that end collected over £250 within a year.

13 The present village police station is well known. In the past it has occupied premises in 1) The West End, 2) The Brae, 3) Where Mrs Giannandrea's cafe is now.

14 A group of weavers' cottages, long since vanished and occupying a piece of the same ground, was once called Balaklava Street.

15 It was versus Bridge of Allan.

16 In May 1981 the club went on to achieve further distinction by winning the West of Scotland Amateur Cup at Hampden Park, and in doing so created a record which almost certainly will never be surpassed. No other club has ever won all three major trophies.

17 Cambusbarron Cooperative Society, after a prosperous beginning when over £1,000 profits were divided amongst members was eventually absorbed into the larger Stirling Society. This happened after a long, bitter and financially onerous rivalry with Messrs. Cullen, butchers, Chapelcroft, had resulted in legal action over a right of way. The butchers' had attempted to prevent co-op access to an alleged right-of-way in the Chapelcroft which the latter needed for transporting stock to the back of their premises (which fronted the Brae). The litigation was the climax of some years of feuding.

18 Woman's Social and Political Union.

APPENDIX

Property	Tenant	Value		
Murrayswood	Thos. Gibson &			
	Arch. Thomson	£29	7	1
West Shillbrae	Thos. Davie	24	10	9
Easter Shillbrae	Alan Jaffrray	24	10	9
Drumshogle	Thos. Touch	24	17	9
Over Castlehill	Andrew Wingate	28	8	8
Glasfearie	Jas. Jenkins	10	10	4
Woodside	John Archibald	19	5	6
Woodside and				
Thorneyhill	Alex. Jamieson	23	19	0
Brownshill	John Johnstone	11	6	9
Nether Castlehill	Alex Murray	21	16	8
Murrayshall	Mrs Wilsone	46	12	0
Wallstale	Jas. Ferguson	28	1	0
Graysteal	Robert Taylor	18	10	4
Newpark	Wm. Archibald	17	10	9
Newpark	Robert Taylor	18	8	3
Newpark	Jas. Crawford	20	17	8
Park Milne and				
Lands	John Archibald	45	3	0
Caldom Hill	Archibald			
	Marshall Tanner	36	16	0
Haggs Burnsdale,				
Easter and				
Wester Cocksethill	John Wordie	50	16	7
Bearside	Helen Jarvie	14	10	5
Bearside	John Davie	11	13	3
Bankend and Slates	John Watson &			
	Robert Downie	22	15	7
Newpark	Andrew McCulley	13	3	2
Broomyknowes and				
Middlehill	Andrew Adam	26	6	3
Gateside	Alex Ure	14	14	7
Kipmad	Patrick Stevenson &			
	Nical Bryce	27	18	0
Cambusbarron Milne				
and Lands	Jas. Neilson	21	0	7
Bridgend of				
Touchadam	Archibald Marshall	2	12	4
The Under Miller's				
Park at Parkmiln	Wm. Telford	3	6	7
Touchadam Muir	Thos. Davie &			
	Alex. Jaffrray	44	6	3
Westertoun	Henry Murdoch	31	6	6
Westertoun	Wm. Murray	37	19	7
Westertoun	Robert Adam	32	15	0
Newmilns	Andrew Mitchell	13	10	4
Newmilns	Wm. Aikman	13	10	4
Hilton	Robert Blair	45	11	4
Hilton	Alex. Henry	54	18	6
Eastertoun	Robert Watt	27	14	4
Eastertoun	Jas. Arthur	27	14	4
Scotstoun	Wm. Watt	28	1	1
Hedding Ford	Alex. Easson	5	5	1
Scotstoun	Alex. McDougall	28	1	0
Longlath	Joseph Henderson	19	5	6
Broomhill	John Christie	11	19	8

Property	Tenant	Value		
Standhill	Wm. Murray	7	6	0
Todhals	Alex. McLay	16	17	8
Bellstones	Thos. McLuskie	26	6	3
Ling	Joseph Russell	13	3	1
Murraysfield	John Ure	8	15	4
Balquidorick	John Robin	21	5	9
Kerse Milne and Lands	John Lamb	115	14	0
The Hole	Henry Edmond	54	6	11
Broomrig	Robert Wingate	61	7	0
Orchyeard	John Kirkwood	20	2	5
Orchyeard	Jas. Hill	24	1	0
Corsepatrick	Jas. McFarlane	92	0	6
Milnhall	Wm. Gillepsie	28	17	7
Dikesamiling	Alex. Watt	36	1	4
Upper Johnstone	Robert Lewis	67	6	7
Middle Johnstone	Jas. McFarlane	40	12	9
Nether Johnstone	Robert Lewis	22	11	10
Risk and Ribbald	Alex. Watt	37	6	10
Newmailing	Alex. Galloway	29	4	2
Lochenair	John Monteath	2	18	5
Hills of Balquinderock	Andrew McGowan	22	15	0
Nether Park of Locheneur	Arch. Marshall	31	11	0
Backcroft) Haypark) Wellcroft) Thornycroft) Pondercroft) Bennyscroft)	Arch. Marshall	91	17	5
Utter Pearl of Locheneur	John Monteath	28	18	6
Sheeppark	John Monteath	12	14	4

Lands in Murray's own possession:

Property		Value		
Bennyhill		31	11	0
Middlepark and Powmaise		19	8	0
Utter Park of Powmaise		35	15	5
Cornquarter of Powmaise		39	5	7
Horseward of Powmaise		10	1	6
Meadow and Long Walk		28	17	6
Orchyeard Gardens and Calfward		17	19	3
Part of Hills of Balquiderock		9	12	11
Tenement and Yeard at St. Ninians (ground only)			8	8
House and Yeard adjoining		1	3	0
Ground House also there		2	9	
Ground of tall houses and yeards at the laigh bridge over Bannockburn Water on road to Powmaise		8	8	
Broomrig		2	12	6
Hills of Balquiderock (part)		4	7	8
Weaving lands of Barrowmeadow		1	15	0
Two acres of Parkside		3	10	1
Damside of Dambends (Cambusbarron)		26	13	10
Clayhills (Cambusbarron)		12	0	0
extending in whole to:		2421	5	10